managing stress

Skills in Action

managing stress
live long and prosper

Dr Derek Roger
Reader in Psychology, University of York

CIM Publishing

CIM Publishing

The Chartered Institute of Marketing
Moor Hall
Cookham
Berkshire
SL6 9QH

www.cim.co.uk

First published 1997
Second edition published 2002
© CIM Publishing 2002

British Library Cataloguing in Publication Data
A CIP catalogue record for this book can be obtained from the British Library.

ISBN 0 902130 60 9

The publishers believe that the contents of this book contribute to debate and offer practical advice. No responsibility will be taken by the publishers for any damage or loss arising from following or interpreting the advice given in this publication.

It is the publisher's policy to use paper manufactured from sustainable forests.

Typesetting by Columns Design Ltd., Reading, Berkshire.
Printed and bound by The Cromwell Press, Trowbridge, Wiltshire.
Cover design by ABA Associates, Ascot, Berkshire.

about the author

Derek Roger is Reader in Psychology in the Department of Health Sciences at the University of York. He set up the 'Challenge of Change' programme of practical stress management, and in 1992 established the Work Skills Centre consultancy. He has worked with a wide range of public and private sector organisations, giving regular presentations to the BBC and NHS Trusts. His practical work has reduced sickness absence and increased job satisfaction and morale in both public and private sector companies and the findings from the studies have been widely published in both the academic and professional press. *Managing Stress* was first published in 1997 and has been extensively revised, rewritten and expanded for this new edition.

acknowledgements

I am very pleased that The Chartered Institute of Marketing has decided to publish a revised version of my book on stress. The techniques described here are offered mainly in the context of dedicated training programmes, and the book gives the opportunity to make the work available to a much wider audience.

The approach to stress described in the book is very different from conventional stress management, and the training is based on a long-term programme of research. These ideas are not always easy to convey, and the editorial contribution from CIM Publishing has been invaluable.

Derek Roger
January 2002

the work skills centre

The Work Skills Centre is an independent consultancy established to provide a vehicle for the implementation of a unique training programme in stress management entitled the Challenge of Change, which is the subject of this book. The Centre is directed by Dr Derek Roger, who has been actively involved in research and training in stress management for the past 16 years. The Centre is staffed by a training team and a programme co-ordinator. The work focuses primarily on individual personal and professional development, but the Centre has established links with other consultancies and is able to offer a comprehensive range of training skills, including an accreditation scheme for the Challenge of Change.

contents

1

the challenge of change

Stress regularly makes headline news, and estimates of the costs of stress to industry in terms of days lost through sickness absence run to millions of pounds annually. However, for all the media coverage, the average reader is still left in the dark as to what exactly stress is. The majority of the press reports imply that stress is caused by external factors, such as family problems, negative equity or bosses demanding productivity targets which people feel are impossible to achieve.

The problem with defining stress in this way is that it becomes an inevitable part of life, since so many of the people we have to deal with or the things which happen to us cannot be avoided or changed. No wonder there is such a strong idea that stress is inevitable and even a good thing: we can 'thrive on stress'.

This book will take the opposite view, and will argue that the only consequence of stress is a miserable and possibly shorter life. This is not to say that our lives should be without pressure, but pressure is not the same as stress. Unfortunately the word 'pressure' does tend to have negative connotations, and it is perhaps more useful to speak of a vacuum which we constantly work into: there is always work to be done, and deadlines are tighter at some times than at others.

However, no job is inherently stressful. What makes it stressful is our **attitude** towards it. While we may not be able to change our jobs or our bosses, we can certainly change our attitudes towards them.

This doesn't mean that external factors should simply be accepted fatalistically, but as we shall see, tackling difficult issues

tackling difficult issues can be done without incurring stress. **The goals are attainable,** provided the principles offered by this book are put into practice.

can be done without incurring stress. The programme for change offered by this book is therefore an optimistic one, and the goals are attainable, provided the principles are put into practice.

One of the major shortcomings of conventional stress management is the absence of any real evidence for the claims that are made. Studies of the effects of stress management seldom meet the criteria for properly controlled scientific research, which would include assessing baseline stress levels before training, having genuine control groups with which to compare the trained participants, and using appropriate statistical analyses to show that any obtained effects were significant. The Challenge of Change training system is based on an ongoing research programme directed by the author, and the findings have been widely published in the scientific press. The research on which the training is based of the system will be presented in Session 2.

Given the misunderstandings there are about stress and stress management, it is important to begin by putting them into perspective, and Session 3 will examine the basis for conventional approaches to managing stress. Part of this traditional approach emphasises signs and symptoms, and indeed, stress is often defined in terms of symptoms. Unfortunately, symptoms tell you very little about causes, and it is the cause of stress that needs to be understood if a cure is to be effected. Because the range of individual symptoms is so great, it is also very difficult to diagnose day-to-day stress. This may not be the case with post-traumatic stress, which occurs after exposure to extreme distress, but these major events are fortunately relatively infrequent, and the focus of this book is on day-to-day stress.

given the misunderstandings there are about stress and stress management, it is important to begin by putting them into perspective

Conventional stress management also emphasises relaxation, but tends to focus on releasing symptoms of tension in the body. Since these have originated mainly in the mind, physical relaxation alone offers symptomatic relief rather than cure, and the programme described here will include relaxation of the mind as well as of the body.

Session 4 focuses on two of the key features of the programme: **waking up** and **controlling attention**. Without taking the first step of waking up, nothing will happen at all, but the emphasis initially is on the inefficiency which results from being asleep much of the time – stress itself is introduced only by the addition of negative emotion to the loss of attention control.

The next step is to know something about yourself, particularly your strengths and liabilities in relation to stress. The Challenge of Change system began as a research project aimed at identifying those aspects of personality and coping that either protected people or made them vulnerable to stress. The research is ongoing, and has led to the development of a series of questionnaires that can be used to quantify specific aspects of personality and coping styles. People vary widely in their personal resources, and knowing what these are allows a much more focused way of beginning to manage stress. Global impressions of 'being stressed' are of little use – what is needed is a precise profile of strengths and liabilities, so that the work can be targeted on changing those habitual ways of behaving that are likely to make people more vulnerable.

global impressions of 'being stressed' are of little use – what is needed is a **precise profile** of strengths and liabilities

Prior to participating in the training, all participants complete a questionnaire that includes a number of these measures, and their scores are used to generate a confidential profile. If you would like to assess some of the key features in the profile, a series of questions can be found in the Appendix, together with instructions for completion and scoring. These will give you your scores on two personality styles and one coping strategy.

You should respond as honestly and as quickly as possible to the questions, and it is essential that these should be completed and scored **before** reading Chapters 4 and 5 – if you know what is being measured, there is the chance that your answers will be biased!

It is important to bear in mind that questionnaires are never perfectly accurate – there is always some degree of error. For example, the questions are intended to assess how you typically react, but a particular question might be biased by the effect of an unusual recent experience. For this reason, the three dimensions that are included in the questionnaire each comprise 10 questions, to minimise the bias that may come from just asking one or two. The score you obtain will range from 0 to 10, and there is no ideal score. Instead, scores are described as high, medium or low, with low scores ranging from 0 to 2 and high from 8 to 10. Depending upon the particular dimension, either a high or a low score might be preferable.

The two personality styles included in the questionnaire are described in detail in Session 5, together with three other relevant aspects of personality. Two coping strategies are described in Session 6, including the one in the questionnaire in the Appendix. They all assess tendencies to behave in particular ways that the research programme has shown are implicated in stress. However, these tendencies are for the most part habits that have become established in us, which means that with practice they can be changed.

It is widely acknowledged that where there is poor communication there is stress, and that where there is stress there is poor communication. The two are closely connected, and in order to break the cycle and to help place the training programme into the wider context of management strategies, Session 7 concentrates on communication. We shall discover there that the same principles used in stress management apply equally to communication skills, and again a contrast is drawn between the conventional 'rules and tools' approach to communication skills training and the approach offered by this book.

The key features are that criticism does nothing but destroy – there is no such thing as 'constructive criticism' – and that effective communication requires a distinction between people and the roles or work they perform. The final session of the book outlines a relaxation technique which has three distinct applications: deep relaxation, rapid relaxation, and relaxing the mind.

these tendencies are for the most part habits that have become established in us, which means that with practice they can be changed

Perhaps a final word before you begin is that reading the book is only the first step. For there to be real change, the principles described here must first be seen as reasonable, since you are unlikely to practice anything you find unreasonable. Secondly, and most importantly, it requires repeated practice. Nothing of value is obtained without effort, and the effort has to be sustained until

the reason we persist with anything is for the goal it offers, and the goal here is nothing less than avoiding a short, miserable life

the old habits are transformed into new and more useful ones. The reason we persist with anything is for the goal it offers, and the goal here is nothing less than avoiding a short, miserable life.

The book proceeds with a brief overview of the research on which the training is based, which is a particular strength of the system. This is then followed in Session 3 by a review of conventional approaches to stress management, in which stress is often defined in terms of symptoms or life events. The shortcomings of these ideas will be pointed out, but without immediately offering an alternative definition. In fact, stress is defined in the Challenge of Change programme as a pre-occupation with emotional upset, and the reasons for this new definition will emerge as the account of the programme unfolds in Session 4.

the research foundation of the training system

One of the strengths of the stress management training system described in this book is the firm foundation in an ongoing programme of scientific research. All too often training packages are based on little more than intuition, and when properly tested, the claims made for their effectiveness often prove baseless.

The work that culminated in the Challenge of Change training system began in 1986 as a research project aimed at discovering why some people were less vulnerable to stress than others. At this stage, there was no specific training application in mind. The goal was simply to find out what it was that seemed to protect some people against stress, and what made others vulnerable. It is widely believed that stress contributes to illness, and the research was also aimed at showing precisely how stress and health were linked together.

the link between stress and health

In fact, the link between stress and illness is by no means straightforward, and is made more complicated by the lack of accurate measurement tools. Stress in particular has proved extremely difficult to assess, and widely used techniques such as life-event scales have proved unreliable (these problems are discussed in detail in Session 3, where the shortcomings of conventional stress management are described). Surprisingly, it is equally difficult to obtain an accurate index of illness. For example, you might consult GP records to find out how many times someone has visited their doctor, but people have very different thresholds for deciding to do so. For some, the first symptom of a cold or flu will be enough, while others will need to feel really ill before doing anything about it. Consulting their records would wrongly suggest that the first group were more ill than the second.

personality and stress

These differences between people in their thresholds for reporting illness provided a hint that personality might be one of the factors involved in linking stress and illness. Personality is defined in a number of different ways, but in this book it will be used to describe the relatively permanent set of characteristics that make us the way we are. The degree to which they are permanent depends upon how they are determined – for example, characteristics such as eye colour are fixed, whereas our beliefs and attitudes depend upon background and experience, and can certainly change. What accounts for the difference between eye colour and attitude is the extent to which genetic factors play a role, and the greater the genetic influence, the more permanent the characteristic.

differences between people in their thresholds for reporting illness provided a hint that personality might be one of the factors involved in linking stress and illness

This is not to say that attitudes are free of genetic influence – indeed, it is probably true that genes have some influence on almost all of our make-up. Personality characteristics tend to be rather mixed, with some having a considerably greater genetic contribution than others. This has important implications for the wider application of the research, since relatively fixed characteristics are unlikely to respond to training. However, the personality factors that are central to the Challenge of Change programme have been shown to be changeable, provided the principles are put into practice (these aspects of personality implicated in stress are described in detail in Session 5).

emotional 'style': a key factor in the stress response

The research programme began by focusing on emotion, and in particular on whether or not experienced emotion was expressed. There is plenty of evidence to show that expressing emotion can help to relieve distress, and the process of counselling is based in part on the unburdening effect of doing so. However, at the time the research began there were few reliable questionnaires available for assessing the tendency to express or inhibit emotion, and the first step was to develop one using a statistical technique known as factor analysis. This is not the place for a detailed description of the procedure, but suffice to say that factor analysis identifies clusters of questions on personality questionnaires that have something in common with one another. Thus if you had a collection of items measuring two quite different things, such as extraversion and anxiety, factor analysis would group the extraversion items onto one cluster (or factor) and the anxiety items onto another.

> there's **plenty of evidence** to show that **expressing emotion** can help to relieve distress, and the process of **counselling** is based in part on the unburdening effect of doing so

The result of this exercise was the Emotion Control Questionnaire or ECQ, which included two distinct emotional 'styles' – emotional inhibition and emotional rumination (the interested reader can find references to articles describing the ECQ in the further reading list at the end of the book). As the name implies, inhibition refers to the tendency to bottle up emotion, while rumination describes the tendency to go on thinking about emotional upset long after the event has passed, or to anticipate upsets in the future. While inhibition did indeed make some contribution to the link between stress and illness, a series of controlled experiments showed that the key to understanding stress was rumination.

When we react to something that is distressing in some way, there is a marked change in our bodies. When we experience this 'fight-or-flight' reaction, our hearts race, our blood

> a **series of controlled experiments** showed that the **key** to understanding stress was **rumination**

pressure increases, and if we're very startled or frightened our hair might stand on end. All of these things are facilitated by changes in the amounts of hormones circulating in the body, especially hormones secreted by the adrenal glands – it is adrenaline, for example, that helps bring about changes in heart-rate and blood pressure. The adrenal glands themselves are stimulated by the combined action of the hypothalamus, found at the base of the brain, and the pituitary gland which is attached to the hypothalamus by a short stalk. These in turn are activated by our interpretation of the environment – our perception of something needing a fight-or-flight response.

Research on stress and health has shown that sustained activation of this hypothalamic-pituitary-adrenal (or h-p-a for short) axis, particularly involving adrenaline and another adrenal hormone, cortisol, is the most likely physiological mechanism for transforming the cognitive perceptions of stress into physical symptoms. When high levels of adrenaline are prolonged, heart-rate and blood pressure remain high, and there is direct stress and strain on the cardiovascular system. Sustained high levels of cortisol, on the other hand, will eventually impair the functioning of the immune system (these processes are described in Session 4, and a more detailed account can be found in references included in the reading list at the end of the book).

These research findings have led to adrenaline and cortisol being referred to as 'stress hormones', but this is not the case: they are simply hormones, performing their intended function. When their levels increase in preparation for fight or flight there is a greater demand on the body's resources, but this is a natural and necessary response to demand. This certainly increases the strain on the body, but as we shall see with simple illustrative examples in Session 4, fight or flight only becomes stressful when there is no opportunity for recovery. Only if the level of arousal is maintained do the beneficial effects of the emergency response become potentially harmful.

fight or flight only becomes stressful when there is no opportunity for recovery

the experimental evidence

The important feature of fight-or-flight is that it begins with a thought, a perception of potential threat or distress. If this were not the case we would respond to everything in the same way. In this context, the new measure of rumination in the ECQ suggested that if the thoughts about things that upset us were to continue after the event so too would the physiological reaction, and this is what the experiments showed. In the first study the participants were exposed to stress in the laboratory, which involved showing them lists of colour words where the words were written in a different colour than the name. For example, the word 'green' was written in brown, and 'yellow' was written in blue. The participants were asked to name the colour the word was written in, and when time pressure was increased the task became increasingly stressful. This can be seen physiologically – the participants' heart-rate and blood pressure were monitored throughout the task, and as the time constraints increased, so did pulse rate and blood pressure.

The task was then stopped, and the time taken for the participants' pulse and blood pressure to return to their normal resting level was recorded. The ECQ scores for all participants had been obtained before the experiment, and the results were unambiguous: the higher the score on rumination, the longer it took that person to recover. In the second experiment, the cortisol levels of a group of student nurses were assessed during and after an important written examination, and the difference between the two measures was compared. Again, the results showed that the higher the rumination score, the more pronounced was the cortisol response.

There has been a long series of experiments like this in the research programme, all showing essentially similar effects. People who tend to ruminate about emotional upset take longer to recover, especially if they also tend to bottle up the emotion they experience. They are also more likely to become ill over demanding periods during which they have to adapt and change. It was this research that led to the new definition of stress as a preoccupation

people who **ruminate** about **emotional upset** take **longer to recover**, especially if they also tend to **bottle up** the emotion they experience with emotional upset. In this context, the only role that life events play is in providing things to ruminate about – they are not in themselves stressful. The new definition provides the cornerstone for the Challenge of Change training system described in this book.

personality and stress: the wider picture

Later in the research programme, a number of other features of personality were identified that made people more or less susceptible to stress, including coping styles. Traditionally, coping had been defined in terms of three primary styles: rational coping, avoidance coping and emotional coping. Rational coping describes a strategy for finding a reasonable solution to the problem, perhaps by seeking advice, but when people are suffering from stress they are much more likely to respond emotionally. Emotional coping may help to relieve some of the distress if it is accompanied by expressing emotion, but in the absence of expressing emotion it represents a failure to cope. Avoidance implies turning away from the problem and pretending it just doesn't exist, which certainly won't lead to a solution.

avoidance implies turning away from the problem and **pretending it just doesn't exist,** which certainly **won't lead to a** solution

The new measure of coping developed by the author and his colleagues included both rational and avoidance coping but subsequent research has shown that they are not particularly implicated in the stress response. However, the third dimension that emerged does have a significant protective role. The new dimension describes a process of being able to step back and see situations in perspective, and was called detached coping. Detached coping combined with elements of emotional coping, so that people who score high on the scale are able to detach relatively quickly, while those who score low tend to become emotionally over-involved. Detachment forms a key element of the Challenge of Change, and as we shall see in Sessions 5 and 6, it is the essential third step in the four stages of dealing effectively with stress.

There is a brief questionnaire in the Appendix, and together with the information provided in Sessions 5 and 6, this offers readers the opportunity to gain some insight into their own characteristic ways of behaving. These and other aspects of personality that serve either to increase or to diminish the risks of suffering from stress will be described in these sessions in more detail. A selection of relevant references can also be found at the end of the book.

what stress management is usually about

As we saw in the Introduction, concern about the damaging effects of stress has led to a proliferation of training programmes which claim to offer ways of coping with it. This book focuses on a new approach based on change and how to respond to it, but we shall begin by examining critically the approach used in conventional training.

There are of course many different aspects of traditional stress management, but three in particular tend to feature prominently: **signs and symptoms of stress, life events,** and **relaxation**. Since much of our understanding of stress tends to be based on these principles, they need to be put into perspective before proceeding to a new approach. In this section of the book we will consider each of them in turn.

the signs and symptoms of stress

Concern over signs and symptoms is essentially a concern about diagnosis – being able to detect whether we or our friends or colleagues are suffering from stress. This is more difficult than it seems, but it is important at this stage to distinguish between **post-traumatic stress** and **everyday stress**.

Post-traumatic stress is the aftermath of exposure to circumstances which exceed the individual's capacity for coping – for example, surviving a major disaster, or an accident in which there is loss of life. The consequence is a range of symptoms which are unambiguously related to the event, such as flashbacks, where vivid images and thoughts about the event persistently intrude in the mind, even in the most ordinary circumstances. The experience can be so vivid that all of the emotional distress which accompanied the event itself recurs, triggering a range of both physical and psychological effects. Post-traumatic stress is a recognised psychological disorder which requires professional counselling, and it is fortunate that events of this magnitude are a relatively rare occurrence.

Everyday stress, by contrast, has to do with the continuous effort of responding to the inexorable change which is the only constant in life. For much of the time, this process of adaptation proceeds unnoticed – we simply adapt without considering the effects, provided there is time for body and mind to recover their equilibrium. However, when the opportunities for recovery are few and far between, and when this is compounded by the particular frame of mind which characterises stress, we seem to be struggling constantly just to keep our heads above water.

for much of the time, **the process of adaptation** proceeds unnoticed – we simply adapt **without considering the effects**, provided there is time for body and mind to recover their equilibrium

While the connection between typical symptoms such as flashbacks and major traumatic incidents is unambiguous, in everyday stress there may be no clear connection between the wide range of possible symptoms and their cause. Furthermore, the symptoms of everyday stress vary so widely from one individual to another that any list of symptoms would have to be impractically long if it were to include everything. The process of trying to recall situations which might have brought about our distress simply leads to confusion, and is in any event about something in the past. In fact, the most important thing to remember here is that events are not in themselves stressful. As we shall see, what makes things stressful is the continued preoccupation with the emotional upset which accompanies these events.

It is of course possible to identify symptoms of everyday stress, and it can be useful, provided we do so with caution and we remember that it is **changes in behaviour** which are important. For example, smoking 20 cigarettes a day may simply be a long-standing habit, and have nothing at all to do with stress. On the other hand, if that increases suddenly to 30 or 40 cigarettes a day, that may be a consequence of stress. Hence it is change in behaviour rather than behaviour per se which we should be alert to, and it is useful to group these critical behaviours into broad categories. This is not intended as an exhaustive list, but it is important to be aware of changes in:

events and people are not in themselves stressful. As we shall see, what makes things stressful is the continued **preoccupation** with the emotional upset which **accompanies** these events

patterns of eating and sleeping

A common consequence of stress is disturbed sleep – taking longer to fall asleep, constantly waking at the smallest sound, and perhaps eventually waking 8 hours later but still feeling exhausted. This comes about because of a preoccupation with emotional upset, and paradoxically, we shall see that the solution to the problem is first to wake up! Disturbances in eating patterns are also commonly associated with stress, and as with sleep may go in either direction – eating too much ('comfort eating') or eating too little. In the latter case the problem may even develop into serious eating disorders such as anorexia, which are known to be affected by stress. Changes in eating patterns can be doubly problematic, since the associated physiological changes also have the effect of interfering with the proper digestion of food.

smoking or alcohol consumption

We have already used the habit of smoking to show how an increase in smoking may be a response to stress. Perhaps a more obvious example is the abuse of alcohol, which is commonly used to combat stress. Unfortunately, it works! After a few drinks, the stress which had previously been foremost in one's mind undoubtedly

a more obvious example is the **abuse of alcohol**, which is commonly used **to combat stress. Unfortunately, it works!**

iᴠᴍ

*what alcohol offers is **oblivion**, which has nothing to do with stress management*

recedes. However, if you are going to use alcohol to combat stress it would be better to stay drunk, because when you sober up things will either be exactly the same or more likely a great deal worse. What alcohol offers is oblivion, which has nothing to do with stress management.

short-temperedness and irritability

A useful way of thinking about short-temperedness and irritability is to see them in the context of attention and attention control. We shall be dealing with this topic in more detail later on, but a simple example will suffice at this point. Let's suppose that you're halfway through a piece of work, but you are interrupted by some other task which needs to be done. You take on the new task, but the unfinished one continues to compete for your attention. If someone then makes a further demand, one possible reaction is irritability and anger. This is not necessarily irritation with that individual (though you may express it that way!) but irritation at having another demand on your attention, which is already divided between two tasks and is compounded by your concern at not being able to give your attention properly to either of them. It is a short step from irritability to short-temperedness to outright anger.

anxiety and depression

Anxiety and depression are readily associated with stress. Although we usually think about them as distinct problems, they seldom occur on their own. More typically, we experience increased mood swings from the one to other, but they do tend to be associated with different time perspectives: as a general rule, anxiety reflects a concern about future events, while depression focuses on regrets

*worrying about the past and the future **changes nothing**, and robs us of the only real time – the present – to give attention to what is in front of us **now***

about the past. As we shall see, merely worrying about the past and the future changes nothing, and robs us of the only real time – the present – to give attention to what is in front of us now.

absent-mindedness and daydreaming

Absent-mindedness and daydreaming are a central feature of the Challenge of Change programme which this book describes. Indeed, what we shall be arguing later on is that we are asleep most of the time, and that if we are to do anything constructive at all, the first step must be to wake up. You have yet to be convinced that you are asleep most of the time, but for this we shall have to await later sessions! What we will discover is that much of our so-called waking state may be spent in nothing more than idle dreaming, and that stress occurs when this idle dream becomes a nightmare.

tiredness, lack of enthusiasm

Tiredness and apathy are symptoms of stress which we're all familiar with. Again, this will be explained later by the paradox of being asleep much of the time, but this is not the restful calm of deep sleep – rather, it is the

> a lack of enthusiasm is an inevitable consequence of the twin demons of non-communication and mis-management

emotional turmoil of nightmares. We shall also see that a lack of enthusiasm is an inevitable consequence of the twin demons of non-communication and mis-management.

susceptibility to illness

It is widely believed that stress causes illness. This is shown in the simple diagram below, where the arrow represents a causal relationship (the more stress you experience the more ill you become):

STRESS   →   ILLNESS

The reverse is also true – illness itself generates feelings of worry and distress, creating a spiral from which it can be difficult to escape. However, there is a problem which arises from equating stress and illness. On the left-hand side of our equation is stress, but what this book will show is that stress is in fact no more than an idea – stress exists almost entirely in the mind. By contrast, the right-hand side of the equation, illness, is an actual change in the physical state of the body, which may lead to an early death.

The question of how an idea, a mere thought, can become a life-threatening condition is one which must be addressed, and we shall be returning to it in a later session. At this stage all we need do is to acknowledge that stress may indeed contribute to illness, and may well shorten your life. There is also no question that what we experience under stress is misery, ranging from irritability or just feeling fed up, to hopelessness, uncontrolled anger or despair. Putting these two points together, what stress leads to is a short, unhappy life, and the paradox is that we actually choose it. As we shall see, stress is not thrust upon us. After all, if that were true there would be no such thing as stress management, since so many of the things which we call stressful are impossible to avoid – managing stress is not about escaping from the world!

There is little more that needs to be said about the signs and symptoms of stress. As we know, there is an almost infinite variety of signs and symptoms of everyday stress, and no list could hope to be comprehensive. However accurate the list, it remains nothing more than a compendium of outward signs and symptoms, which in themselves will not lead us any closer to the causes of stress – only in cases of post-traumatic stress can we be confident about the link between symptoms and cause. It is useful to have a general sense of what people might experience when they are under stress, provided there is a clear distinction between those which may be a consequence of stress and those which are simply long-standing habits.

The simplest way to resolve this problem is to look for changes in the way people behave – take what you first observe as the baseline, and work from there. The list of seven broad categories of symptoms provided in this chapter can then be seen for what it is – not a diagnostic manual but a general indication of where change might be cause for concern.

life events

A second pillar of conventional stress management is the belief that events are in some sense inherently stressful. This view is exemplified by the so-called 'life events' approach to defining stress. We have probably all seen copies of life event scales in magazines and newspaper articles – lists of things which might happen to us in everyday life, ranging from the death of someone close to us, to going on holiday. Life event scales typically comprise between 60 and 100 events, and the table below shows some sample items from a typical scale (we shall say more about the readjustment scores later).

life event scales: some sample items

event	mean readjustment score
Death of someone close to you	100
Divorce	73
Personal injury/illness	53
Marriage	50
Retirement	45
Change in financial status	38
Son/daughter leaving home	29
Moving house	28
Change in sleeping patterns	16
Vacations	13
Christmas	12

What you are asked to do with these scales is to tick those events which have **actually** happened to you in the past, say, six months. Clearly, in many Western cultures, if such a scale is completed in February, most people are likely to tick Christmas! The principle that these scales are based on is that we all have a capacity for coping or adapting. Any event which occurs in our lives requires a degree of adaptation, and will consequently make some demand on our capacity. The life events approach

> the
> life events approach argues
> that if enough events occur, **our
> capacity for adaptation may
> become exhausted** and we
> then suffer from stress

argues that if enough events occur, this capacity may become exhausted, and we then suffer from stress.

It is not difficult to see the fallacy in this approach to stress. For example, just as with signs and symptoms of stress, no life event scale could possibly be comprehensive. You may have a scale with a hundred items, but one individual may have experienced twenty events which don't happen to appear on your scale. If it were true that the number of events ticked off did indicate how stressed people were, then in this case the scale would be entirely misleading. Another problem with life events is that things may happen to people because they have become ill – for example, someone may have retired because of illness. This turns back-to-front our view that the stress of the event causes illness!

Life event scales also assume that these events have a similar impact for all individuals. Simple observation of the victims of major disasters tells us otherwise – even in extremely traumatic circumstances, different people respond in different ways. To take another example, one of the items commonly listed in life event scales is 'divorce'. Conventionally, there are two main players in a divorce, husband and wife. For one of these partners the divorce may be an absolute disaster, the beginning of the end; for the other, it may be freedom at last. Clearly, we cannot assume an equal impact on both of them.

In an attempt to overcome some of these and other criticisms, life event scales have been modified in various ways to allow a more refined assessment of the impact of the events. For example, a life event scale with 'death of spouse' at the top was given to a large sample of married subjects. A score of 100 was given to this event, which was assumed to be the most stressful thing these people could experience. All of the remaining events were then entered randomly and without any scores, and the subjects were asked to give a score to each event based on the notional benchmark maximum of 100 for death of spouse.

> life
> **event scales assume**
> that these events have a similar
> impact for all individuals – **but even in**
> traumatic circumstances, **people
> respond in different
> ways**

The 'mean readjustment scores' opposite the sample items in the table above represent the average scores which were given to these events. This technique was supposed to provide a more accurate and sensitive index of stress, a kind of 'stress quotient'. However, subsequent research has shown that there is no difference in sensitivity, regardless of whether ticks or scores are used, and the problems discussed above still apply.

> the **problem** with the life events approach lies in suggesting that stress is the property of events, and that events are therefore **inherently stressful**

Quite apart from these issues, the most important problem with the life events approach lies in suggesting that stress is the property of events, and that events are therefore inherently stressful. If you take this approach, you have no choice but to resign yourself to a life of stress. After all, most of the events which affect us simply happen, and trying to structure your life to avoid certain events and people would in itself be stressful! A different approach is to assume that there is in fact no such thing as a stressful event, only a stressful way of responding to events. Stress, then, is in the mind, and this offers a way out – you may not be able to change events, but you can certainly change your mind.

relaxation

Finally, conventional stress management tends to include relaxation. As we shall see, relaxation is helpful, but it is not of itself stress management. This is because physical relaxation works primarily at the level of the body, and the body is after all no more than flesh and blood: it does what it does only because of the activity of the mind. Any tension in the body is therefore a reflection of tension in the mind. The body does not become tense of its own accord, and in this respect what happens in the body is often a symptom of activity in the mind. Of course, when we become

> the **body does not become tense of its own accord**, and in this respect what happens in the body is often a **symptom** of activity **in the mind**

aware that our bodies are tense we may then become more anxious or upset, creating a cycle of tension, but the physical changes in the body are essentially brought about by an appraisal of something in the mind.

In this view, relaxation is useful but must merely be palliative until the mind is relaxed as well. To use a simple example, one might learn to relax completely, so much so that arriving at one's desk in the morning, one can sit down and be completely free of tension. The first job then arrives, but is unfortunately of the 'oh no, not that again!' variety. Immediately all of the physical tension returns. So, relaxation is important, but it deals primarily with symptoms. What this book is concerned with is not symptoms but causes, since it is only by tackling the cause that we can hope to effect a cure.

learning points from session 3

- Listing signs and symptoms of stress does not offer a cure. The symptoms of stress are not in themselves the problem, they simply present **outward signs of inner conflict**.
- In any event, the link between the cause and the symptom is often unclear in the case of everyday stress – only in post-traumatic stress are the causes and the symptoms unambiguously linked. This book focuses primarily on dealing with everyday stress, and is explicitly **preventative** in its approach.
- It is possible to identify symptoms of everyday stress, but such a 'diagnosis' should be made with great caution and should be based on **changes** in behaviour.
- Events are **not in themselves stressful**. If they were, then everyone would respond in the same way to the same event, and they don't. Taking the view that events are in some sense inherently stressful may provide convenient targets for blame, but it offers no way out of stress, since you can do little to avoid the people and things which come your way.
- Relaxation can be a useful tool, **but is not of itself stress management**. Relaxation deals primarily with tension in the body, which is a symptom of activity in the mind. To manage stress successfully, we must address the cause and not just the symptom.

4

what the challenge of change programme is about

waking up

We have already said that the first step is to wake up. What do we mean by this?

The problem with ideas about being awake and being asleep is that, as with most things, we tend to think in twos. So we imagine that when we go to sleep at night that is sleep, until we wake up in the morning. We are then awake until we go to sleep again the following night. Now look at the diagram below.

WIDE AWAKE
|
WAKING SLEEP
|
SLEEPWALKING
|
DREAMING SLEEP
|
DEEP SLEEP

Fig. I

At the top and the bottom of this diagram are these two states of wide awake and deep sleep. If we consider deep sleep first, there are certainly periods during the night when we all experience deep sleep (it may not always feel like it, particular when we're under pressure!) In this state of deep sleep people become quite still, they are difficult to wake up, and their pattern of 'brain waves', measured by an electro-encephalogram (EEG) is dramatically different from the ordinary waking state.

However, during the course of the night we also experience dreaming sleep, whether or not we subsequently remember the dreams. We know when someone is dreaming from the pattern of their eye movements, since in dreaming sleep there are 'rapid eye movements' (REM) when the eyes flicker under the lids. When people are no longer in deep sleep they may also become restless, so there is an increase in physical movement. They are easier to wake up than in deep sleep and the pattern of brain activity from the EEG trace is much more like the waking state. So, what we have thought of as a single state, sleep, is in fact a continuum. The next level in this continuum is sleep-walking, where a person may get up, walk about the house, and perform complex activities. Brain activity shows a pattern which is in fact indistinguishable from the waking state, and yet we still call this person asleep!

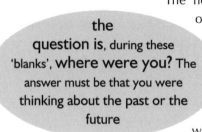

the question is, during these 'blanks', where were you? The answer must be that you were thinking about the past or the future

The next step on the continuum is our ordinary waking state, but here it is called waking sleep. Take a simple example: you are driving down a motorway and you get to junction 20. The next thing you know you are at junction 25, with no recollection of anything between those junctions. Or you find yourself behind your desk with no memory of getting up, washing or having breakfast. Worst of all, you get up on a lazy Sunday and head off to play golf and the next thing you find yourself arriving in front of your office! The question is, during these 'blanks', where were you?

The answer must be that you were thinking about yesterday or tomorrow, the past or the future. The future is plainly a complete fantasy, but the past is equally so – we are extremely selective about what we remember. For example, yesterday's argument which you lost is magically transformed today between junctions 20 and 25 into one that you resoundingly win! The past is filtered through our perceptions and becomes personal, an invention of hindsight that may have little objective reality – two adult siblings recalling the experience of their childhood will often give accounts so different they might have grown up in different families. In fact, what we call 'my life' is mostly a story made up by selectively remembering – and usually embellishing to suit our image of ourselves.

If all this is fantasy it must simply be a dream, and if it is a dream we must still be asleep. The fact that we're driving down the motorway at 70 miles an hour doesn't mean we're awake – when we sleep-walk we perform equally complex tasks on 'auto pilot', and we have no hesitation in saying that a sleep-walker is asleep. This is one reason why accidents occur – drivers in 'waking sleep' simply don't wake up quickly enough to respond in time.

the difference between 'waking sleep' and intentional behaviour

Of course, it may be appropriate to go into the past and the future, provided it is **intentional**. For example, the piece of work arriving on your table may require some forward planning or drawing on experience, but going into the past or future in this case is done by intentionally giving attention. In the same way, the building you may be sitting in while you read this is first formed as an idea in the mind of an architect. He or she may draw on past experience to decide which materials to use and will have some plan about what the building will eventually look like when it is finished. At that stage the building is a dream based on past experience and expectation, but the architect's attention is under control – it is **given**, not snatched away by the past or the future.

The final stage of our continuum is wide awake. One way to illustrate being wide awake is to return to our motorway example. Let's suppose that between junctions 20 and 25 we are engrossed in the dream of the past or the future. There is suddenly an accident ahead, but on this occasion, we wake up in time. Many people have a similar experience of these circumstances – there is no time to think about what we read in the *Times* about

> people who behave **appropriately** in emergencies are described as having **presence of mind**, and we should interpret this literally – **their mind is in the present**

someone's behaviour in an emergency and try to follow suit. Instead, the mind becomes completely clear, and attention is given fully to the event as it unfolds in front of us, often seemingly in slow-motion. People who behave absolutely appropriately in emergencies are described as having presence of mind, and we should interpret this literally – their mind is in the present, rather than absentmindedly wandering about in the past or the future.

The first step in the challenge of change is waking up – not being shocked awake but waking up and intentionally staying awake. This is essential if we are to work efficiently – after all, you cannot work and sleep simultaneously. You need only consider for a moment how much time in a 24-hour period you spend from waking sleep downwards on our diagram to realise just how inefficient we can be. And what's more, this is just idle dreaming – we have yet to introduce stress!

controlling attention

The diagram below shows a quasi-computer model comprising (i) an event, (ii) a cross-section through someone's head containing a box labelled mind, (iii) an input channel taking information via the sense organs to the mind, and (iv) an output channel taking attention from the mind back to the event.

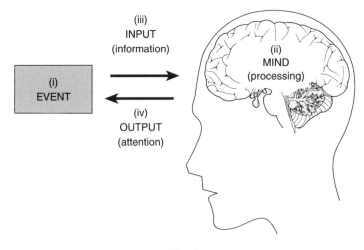

Fig. 2

In the diagram, the event represents anything in the world outside, such as a piece of work you have to do or a person you are meeting. Whatever the event might be, it provides information which is channelled to the mind for interpretation. We could argue endlessly about what mind is, but for the purposes of our model we have defined it as a **processor of information**. Once the processing has been completed, attention is given via the output channel; indeed, the only 'output' from the mind is attention.

Attention may be expressed in any kind of activity. For example, for this particular piece of work you may have to write something, in which case your attention will be on the content of the message, the co-ordination of your hands, and so on. Or you may have take action which takes you away from your desk altogether, and attention may then be given to walking or driving. Some of this activity may well be carried out on 'auto pilot', but this doesn't mean no attention is being given – all it means is that you're not aware of doing so! On the other hand, some form of mental activity may be required, such as remembering something or thinking about the task. In this case what is attended to is within the mind, but it is nonetheless the giving of attention. If you are asked to remember an event which happened yesterday, it is brought to mind and attended to – you give your attention to what is remembered.

attention given and attention snatched away

Each event which is acted upon progresses and changes, whether the work you do is mental or physical. New information is then available, leading to new processing and attention. In fact, this is how all work gets done. Unfortunately, however, the model describes an ideal situation, and in practice things are often rather different. Take a simple example: a piece of work lands on your desk, and your first response is 'oh no, not that again!' What do you do next? In all probability, you begin to think about

a piece of work lands on your desk, and your first response is **'oh no, not that again!'** What do you do next? In all probability, you begin to think about some-thing else

something else. At that point your attention is no longer given to the work in front of you or to some relevant thinking about it; instead, it is captured or caught by whatever the current fantasy happens to be – next weekend, last weekend, next holiday, last holiday, anything except the work. This is shown in the next diagram, where the outward attention is drawn back into the mind by the broken line:

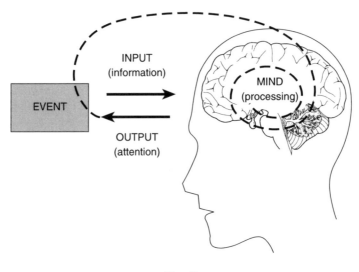

Fig. 3

The broken line ends up circling around some imaginary situation, and this is what waking sleep is about. You are to all intents and purposes there, but your mind is elsewhere – you are literally absent-minded, as opposed to having presence of mind.

It is important to distinguish this experience from the purposeful giving of attention to the past or the future, which we illustrated in the last section with the examples of planning for a task and drawing on experience, or an architect planning a building. In the latter case, he or she will draw on past experience to decide which materials to use, or will go into the future to envisage what the building might eventually look like. This is entirely appropriate, and represents in our model an example of attention controlled and given to an event in the mind. This is quite different from having your attention snatched away by the broken line in the diagram.

the costs of captured attention

The cost of waking sleep is that while your attention is taken by something else, no work gets done – you can't work and sleep at the same time. Reflecting on how much of the time is spent in this state gives an indication of just how inefficient we actually are, and how much more efficient we could be by taking the first steps of waking up and controlling attention.

presence of mind

A simple way to feel the effect of cutting or short-circuiting the broken line is to stop whatever you happen to be doing, and find a comfortable position in the chair. Relax you body as fully as you can, and be aware of your breathing. Relax your chest and stomach fully – let each breath come and go without trying to breathe more deeply or more shallowly. Then close your eyes, and listen to all of the sounds you can hear around you. Begin with the closest sounds in the room. Then let the sense of listening extend outwards to the rest of the building, then outside, then out to the most distant sound you can hear. Try to listen to each sound without letting a picture of what you can hear to form in the mind – try to hear it as just a sound. If any thoughts or ideas from the past or the future come into the mind, notice how they distract your attention from just listening. As soon as you become aware of the thought or idea, connect your attention again with the sounds you can hear. Keep listening for a minute or two, then open your eyes. If you were able to let go of the ideas, even for a short while, you will have noticed a freedom from tension as the mind became still. This is what presence of mind is about.

stress and attention control

But what has this to do with stress? To bring stress into our model we need an added ingredient in our diagrams: **negative emotion**. This is best illustrated by an example. Suppose a piece of work has been brought to you by your supervisor or line manager, who then goes out. The work may be of the 'oh no, not that again' variety, in which case you may well drift off into idle dreaming. Now change the scenario: on this occasion the manager comes in and gives you the work, but turns back at the door

the manager comes in and gives you the work, but turns back at the door and says, **'just do a better job of it this time, right?'** What follows then is **frustration, anger, fear, resentment** – in other words, **negative emotion**

and says, 'just do a better job of it this time, right?' What follows then is frustration, anger, fear, resentment – in other words, negative emotion, and there are two important consequences of adding negative emotion. First of all, the red line that we described earlier as just idle dreaming turns into a nightmare of misery. Everyone ruminating about emotions like fear, anger and resentment must acknowledge that they feel downright miserable.

Secondly, the body is triggered into a physical response called 'fight or flight'. This was described briefly in Session 1, but the process needs to be fully understood because it is the main mechanism that links stress and illness. To recap, at the base of the brain is the hypothalamus, which is connected by a short stalk and a duct to the pituitary gland. The pituitary and hypothalamus in turn communicate with the two adrenal glands, each situated above the kidneys in the small of your back. The adrenal glands have an outer part and an inner part, and for convenience we can think of them as concentric circles, with the outer part called the cortex and the inner part called the medulla. The pathways connecting the pituitary and hypothalamus to the adrenal glands are both neural (nerve) and chemical, and are shown in the diagram below.

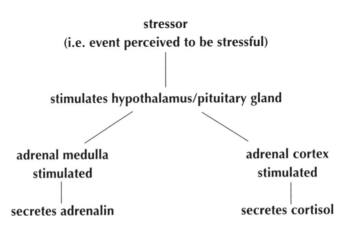

stressor
(i.e. event perceived to be stressful)

stimulates hypothalamus/pituitary gland

adrenal medulla stimulated

adrenal cortex stimulated

secretes adrenalin

secretes cortisol

Fig. 4.

The diagram shows the hypothalamic-pituitary-adrenal axis, or h-p-a, which is preceded by a thought process. When there is a change in the environment, a decision is taken about whether or not a response is needed. It might be something quite expected and unthreatening, but if it is novel or potentially threatening the hypothalamus is stimulated, and it in turn signals the adrenal medulla to secrete large amounts of adrenaline. Adrenaline is always present in the bloodstream, and the level increases in response to anything that requires attention, but the reaction is particularly intense when the event is threatening – hence the term, 'fight or flight'. The effect of this dramatic increase in adrenaline is preparation for action – rapid heart rate, increased blood pressure, rapid, shallow breathing, and a whole range of other effects which are less obvious but which all contribute to the readiness to respond.

Fight or flight is easily illustrated from everyday examples. Imagine you are working quietly and someone drops a large book on the floor behind you. The startled feeling that follows is fight or flight, and if you were sufficiently frightened your hair might stand on end. The reaction seems instantaneous, but remember that the mind has processed the information and decided that this is something to respond to – after all, we don't react in this way to everything that happens, only to things that may be threatening.

The fight or flight reaction certainly makes a huge demand on the body, but it is important not to confuse it with stress. Being able to respond so rapidly to potential threat is adaptive and essential, and represents a highly intelligent process that has evolved to ensure our survival – it is just as well it happens so fast and that we can do little to stop it. However, the body needs time to recover from the demand, so whether or not we become stressed depends upon the length of time it continues. A simple way of linking fight or flight to stress is to use a diagram of a river with a bend in it:

> the fight or flight reaction certainly makes a **huge demand on the body**, but it is important **not to confuse it** with stress. Being able to respond so rapidly to potential threat is **adaptive and essential**

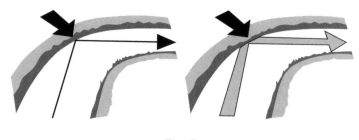

Fig. 5

The flow of water has been shown in the left-hand part of the diagram, with the maximum pressure indicated at the point on the outside bank where the current strikes the bend. The right-hand part of the diagram shows the river in flood – when this happens, the bank will begin to erode and collapse at the point of maximum pressure. Now substitute for the river an artery, your own coronary artery. The coronary artery loops up from the heart and returns to feed the heart muscle itself, and is full of bends and forks. When fight or flight is provoked and the level of adrenaline soars, the effect on the cardiovascular system is equivalent to the flood in the river: a huge increase in heart rate and blood pressure, and direct physical strain on the cardiovascular system.

an illustrative example: the cat on the mat

However, one of the differences between rivers and arteries is that the living body is capable of renewing itself. Our bodies are constantly creating new cells to replace those that die. However, the rate of repair must remain ahead of the rate of damage, and for this there must be a period of recovery. To illustrate with a simple everyday example: suppose you tiptoe up to a pet cat asleep in front of the fire. At the last minute it wakes up and it jumps up into the air, hair standing on end. The cat's reaction is fight or flight, exactly the same as ours to the book dropped unexpectedly behind us. However, a moment later the cat recognises you, and because you're not a threat it relaxes – the excess adrenaline is no longer needed and is quickly metabolised, the cat's heart slows and its hair flattens.

Now what the cat doesn't do is to sit around afterwards thinking, 'that might have been the dog next door! What if I hadn't woken up – I might have died!' Using this example, reflect for a moment on the last time something really upset you. When you bring it fully to mind you identify with it all over again, and if you were linked up to a heart rate monitor your heart rate would increase from the normal level of 70 or 80 beats a minute to something like 100. And if you reflect further, how often and for how long do you go on and on thinking about these sorts of things after they have happened? The effect may not be as intense as when you first experienced it, but each time you do so you trigger fight or flight, in the absence of anything to respond to except an idea in your mind!

If the activation of the body is repeatedly provoked without rest, the damage may become permanent. For example, the inner lining of the arteries is protected by a fine layer of cells which help to prevent the formation of fatty plaques, but once there is damage to the arterial wall the plaque may form and gradually begin to block the blood flow. This is coronary heart disease, a progressive narrowing of the artery until the heart can no longer function and you suffer a heart attack.

> what the cat doesn't do is to sit around afterwards thinking, 'that might have been the dog next door! What if I hadn't woken up – I might have died!'

Furthermore, we saw in the diagram of the h-p-a axis that it is not only the inner medulla of the adrenal gland that is stimulated. The outer part, the cortex, is also activated, and during fight or flight it secretes a range of hormones including cortisol. The synthetic equivalent of cortisol is cortisone, a powerful anti-inflammatory drug. Cortisol has a number of functions, including facilitating the release of stored sugar to provide the energy for fighting or fleeing, but the anti-inflammatory effect is needed to control or limit inflammation if there is actual physical injury during the emergency. Inflammation at the site of the injury is a natural and helpful response, but left to run its course it may eventually restrict blood flow, and cortisol helps to restrain the inflammation.

However, another function of cortisol is to regulate bodily functions, including the production of some white blood cells. When cortisol levels are kept high in experiments, the white blood cell count is found to gradually diminish. White blood cells form the cornerstone of our immune system, and compromising white blood cell production will also compromise immunity. The elevations in cortisol and adrenaline provoked by the fight or flight reaction are not in themselves stressful. They become stressful for the body only if they are unnecessarily sustained, and the way to sustain them is to continue to ruminate about emotional upset. Negative emotional rumination also understandably makes you feel miserable, which is why all that stress (defined specifically as rumination) offers you is nothing other than a miserable and possibly shorter life.

> the **elevations in cortisol and adrenaline** provoked by the fight or flight reaction are not in themselves stressful. They become stressful for the body **only if they are unnecessarily sustained**

roadworks!

There are of course many factors that contribute to serious illnesses such as heart disease, including a poor diet, lack of exercise and especially genetic predispositions. Paradoxically, good genes may give you the one thing worse than a short miserable life – a long miserable one! However, while genetic factors are beyond our control, stress certainly isn't. Blaming others for giving you stress may make you feel better, but it is untrue and serves only to perpetuate the 'blaming culture'. Take a simple example. You're driving to a meeting at 9 o'clock, but having forgotten the roadworks, you turn a corner and find yourself at the back of a motorway queue. You react as if the roadworks were put there especially to annoy you personally, and you fume and rage and blame. You eventually get to work and go on fuming and raging, and make everyone else miserable as well.

> you react as if **the roadworks were put there especially to annoy you personally**, and you **fume and rage and blame**. For all your sound and fury, **what happened to the motorway queue?**

There is a simple question: for all your sound and fury, what happened to the motorway queue? It didn't move an inch. No amount of anger will get you to the meeting on time – all it does is to give you a more miserable life, and is unreasonable and irrational. You could have taken a different route, and the reason you forgot the roadworks may well have been worry about the meeting in the first place! However, having forgotten, nothing is achieved by losing your temper, or by any other kind of emotional outburst either. Which is not to say you don't care about being late, but fear and anger change nothing.

stress is not the event, it is a preoccupation with the emotional upset which follows from the event

Two things should be clear from this. The first is that we need to think again about what stress is. Attributing your feelings of stress to someone or something, be it roadworks or your manager, is a misunderstanding. Stress is not the event, it is a **preoccupation with the emotional upset which follows from the event**. All the event provides is something to ruminate about, if you decide to do so. Secondly, this preoccupation is chosen. However inconvenient, being stuck in a motorway queue is simply an event, and you're not genetically programmed to get angry or upset about it. You can respond in any way you choose, including becoming stressed by adding the ingredient of negative emotion. The window of opportunity in which to make the choice is small, but it is nonetheless there. Knowing what the effect of the unneccesary anger will be, you then have the opportunity to let it all go.

another illustrative example: catching monkeys

Catching monkeys provides a useful analogy for stress and the principle of letting go. If you want to catch a monkey, take a pot with a hole in it just big enough for him to get his hand in. Tie it to the ground, put one peanut inside and hide behind a tree. The monkey comes out, puts his hand in and grabs the peanut. He now has a fist too big to pull back out through the hole, and you run up and catch him. If the monkey looked around he would see that the forest was full of food, but he gives up his life for a single peanut.

all the monkey had to do to be free was to **open his hand**, and this is an appropriate metaphor for our lives

All the monkey had to do to be free was to open his hand and let go, and this is an appropriate metaphor for our lives. In exactly the same way, all we need do in situations like motorway queues is to let go of the negative emotion. As we saw earlier, people who react in exactly the right way in emergencies are described as having presence of mind, which means their minds are in the present. The rage, anxiety and all the rest revolve around 'what if' and 'if only' – what might happen when you eventually get to work, if only you had taken a different route. This is wishful thinking about the past and the future, a dream that negative emotion transforms into a nightmare.

You might respond by saying this is easier said than done, and you would be absolutely right! It is possible to lead a life free of stress, but to do so is much the same as learning to ride a bicycle. You see someone riding expertly, and you jump on – and fall straight off again. You might ask how to do it, and the theoretical advice will help up to a point, but the only way to learn to ride is practice. The same is true of stress management: there are no 'magic bullets'. The information about what stress is and how it affects your body and mind is useful, but will remain theory without practice. Learning to cycle is in effect substituting the habit of not being able to ride for the habit of being able to. With stress, what we have is a collection of habitual ways of responding to things. We need to wake up to the fact that these can change, and that these habitual reactions are not human nature – after all, nothing natural would give you a short miserable life.

one has simply to keep practising, despite the failures along the way. **There are no 'magic bullets'** in stress management

This **is** easier said than done, but it is a short step from there to thinking it is so difficult you can't possibly do it. One has simply to keep practising, despite the failures along the way. As you begin to get your balance on a bicycle you still fall off from time to time, but less and less often, and that's how it is with stress management as well.

learning points from session 4

- The first point is that we tend to be **asleep most of the time**. This is best understood as a continuum of sleep, from deep sleep through dreaming sleep, sleepwalking, and waking sleep to wide awake.

- Waking sleep is characterised by being 'elsewhere', with **attention caught** by some idea from the past or the future. When people behave appropriately in emergencies we describe them as having 'presence of mind'; this means literally that their minds are in the present, rather than absent-mindedly off in the past or the future, and they are really awake.

- The effects of waking sleep are best understood by considering the mind as a processor of information that it receives from events in the world. It then gives attention to the event, and this attention can be given in any form, physical or mental. However, when attention drifts off onto something else, such as plans for next weekend or remembering last weekend, **control is lost** and attention has been snatched away.

- While idle dreaming continues no work is done – it is impossible to work and sleep. However, when the ingredient of **negative emotion** is added, this changes into stress. The mind is then preoccupied with 'what ifs' and 'if onlys', and the experience is misery. In addition, the 'fight or flight' response continues to be provoked each time the event is thought about, with the consequence that adrenaline and cortisol levels remain elevated. This offers an explicit link between stress and illness, and defines stress clearly as a preoccupation with emotional upset. It is not the event but the rumination afterwards that is stressful.

- Examples such as being caught in motorway queues show clearly that there is a **choice** involved, which must be taken during a small window of opportunity before rushing into the mechanical process of anger, fear and the rest. However, to take this step you first have to be awake.

● The analogy of the monkey giving up its life for the sake of a single peanut is a **metaphor for day to day stress** – most of what we worry about is, with hindsight, of little real consequence.

most of what we worry about is, with hindsight, of little real consequence

knowing yourself: personality styles

We noted earlier in this book, when we spoke about stress and its effects, that people respond very differently to the same situation. This is one of the main shortcomings of the life events approach, which regards events as inherently stressful. If this were true then everyone would respond to the same event in the same way, and we used one of the items from the life event scale, divorce, to demonstrate that the implications for the two people involved in it might be very different indeed. We can now take this a step further. If there is a wide range in the way that people respond to events there must be something about individuals which either protects them against stress or makes them more vulnerable, and one of these individual features is **personality**.

We need to be clear about what personality is. As we saw in Session 2, there are two ways of defining personality – as something which is inherited (in other words, which has a biological or genetic basis), or as something which is acquired or learned. There are some aspects of personality which are to a degree genetically determined. In fact, it is probably true that most aspects of our behaviour have at least some genetic component, but it would be useful to view this as a continuum. Using again the example of eye colour, this is clearly genetically determined, and remains the same throughout one's lifetime. At the other extreme, attitudes and preju- dices are unlikely to be determined in this direct way by genes. It may be that a biological or genetic factor contributes in some way to making some people more likely to become prejudiced, but the influence of genetics, if there is any at all, is going to be extremely small. Most personality factors, and certainly the ones we will be examining in the context of stress, will tend to towards the latter end of the genetic continuum.

The second way in which predictable and characteristic personality differences come about is through learning, which depends upon the reinforcement – positive or negative – which accompanies our responses to events. Expressed very simply, when our behaviour is punished in some way we are less likely to repeat it, whereas if it is rewarded we are more likely to repeat it. In this way our responses become shaped and habitual, and even though they are acquired through learning they become predictable aspects of our behavioural repertoire. The aspects of personality which will be discussed in this section are for the most part acquired rather than innate, which is important, since behaviour that has some biogenetic basis will be more difficult to change.

when our behaviour is punished in some way we are less likely to repeat it, whereas if it is rewarded we are more likely to repeat it. In this way **our responses become shaped and habitual**

However, the argument over whether our personality is determined by nature or nurture is in many ways an oversimplification. There can be little doubt that we behave in typical and fairly predictable ways, and that these characteristic responses are determined either genetically or by means of consistent reinforcement, but our behaviour might also change quite dramatically in response to situations. In fact, the way we respond is most likely to be determined by an **interaction** between our predispositions, determined either by genetics or learning, and our reactions to particular situations.

The interactive principle is clearly illustrated in the case of diseases. For example, people differ in their susceptibility to diseases such as tuberculosis, but being genetically susceptible does not mean you will inevitably contract the disease – you will only do so if you are exposed to the bacteria, and it is the interaction between the predisposition and the external agent which leads to illness. In the same way, if you are less genetically vulnerable then even if you are exposed to the agent you are less likely to develop the disease.

Another important point about personality is that in order to know anything about it you have to be able to measure it, and personality is usually assessed by means of scales or questionnaires. The format of the questions will typically be **dichotomised**, where there is a choice between two alternatives ('yes/no', for example, or 'agree/disagree'), or **scaled**, where there is a choice between more than two alternatives (for example, a four-point scale comprising 'always', 'sometimes', 'seldom', and 'never'). The answers are then scored on the basis of a predetermined allocation of points, which in the case of the four-point scale may allocate zero for 'never' through to 3 points for 'always', though the direction of the scoring will naturally vary according to the way the item is phrased. The questionnaire in the appendix employs a dichotomised format, and you were asked to respond by either agreeing or disagreeing with each of the statements.

Questionnaires offer a convenient way of assessing the stable personality predispositions which govern people's behaviour, but it should be borne in mind that they may be affected by a whole range of factors. One of these is 'social desirability' – trying to work out what is being measured and answering in such a way as to present yourself in the best (i.e., the most socially desirable) light. A second problem has a particular effect on dichotomised response formats. Here you are asked to choose between true/false, and in some of these cases you may feel that the statement is neither entirely true nor false – it depends on the situation.

For this reason, the instructions for dichotomised questionnaires should invite an answer in terms of how you **typically** behave, choosing the alternative that is most characteristic of yourself. It is also important to remember that no questionnaire can ever offer an assessment of an individual's personality which is perfectly accurate – it is always only an approximation. At the same time, provided the reliability and validity of a scale has been adequately tested, the score will offer a fair assessment of your characteristic way of responding, and that in turn offers an insight into strengths which can be called upon and liabilities which may need to be addressed.

provided the **reliability** and **validity** of a scale has been adequately tested, the score will offer a **fair assessment** of your characteristic **way of responding**

It is also important to remember that personality factors tend to be normally distributed in the population. This means that the scores will approximate to a bell-shaped curve, where the horizontal axis represents scores along a continuum from lowest to highest and the vertical axis represents numbers of people obtaining those scores. The bell shape implies that the further you go out towards very high or very low scores, the fewer people there are – in other words, for most personality factors, the majority of the population will be clustered around the average. This reflects the view of personality as a **dimension** rather than a typology. Although we often speak of personality 'types', people do not in practice fall into the non-overlapping categories which the term implies.

The scales comprising the short questionnaire in the appendix are not intended to provide a comprehensive account of your personality, and having just ten questions in each of the three scales they provide no more than a 'snapshot' of each dimension. However, the longer questionnaires from which they were derived have all been extensively validated, and the scales measure aspects of personality that are known to be implicated in the stress response. You should find that the scales do reflect your typical way of responding, and the profile which results from them will help you to identify those aspects of your own behaviour which serve either to protect you or to make you more vulnerable to stress.

The questionnaire yields scores on three dimensions, labelled R, E-I and Det. These stand for Rumination, Emotional Inhibition and Detachment, respectively. The first two are measures of personality, while detachment is an index of a particular coping style. Rumination and inhibition will be discussed in this chapter, while detached coping will be described together with another aspect of coping in Session 6. The intention of including these scales as part of the book is to provide some insight into the way you typically react, but because of the biases spoken about earlier they do need to be interpreted with caution. It is also important to remember that these aspects of your behaviour are largely habitual, and they can be changed provided there is the will to do so!

A number of other personality and coping styles are included in the full Challenge of Change training programme. All of the scales are completed and scored before the training sessions, and the full profile of scores and their implications for dealing with stress are discussed in detail during

these aspects of your behaviour are largely habitual, and they can be changed provided there is the will to do so!

the session. No individual scores are ever disclosed, but the confidential profile that results from the exercise provides a focused and specific overview of strengths that can be drawn upon and vulnerabilities that need to change. Although the questionnaire found in the Appendix comprises just three of these scales, five other relevant aspects of personality and coping will be described below and in Session 6.

the questionnaire profile

The scores from the questionnaire in the Appendix comprise the following two personality dimensions:

1. Emotional rumination (R in the appendix). The first scale is a measure of the extent to which individuals tend to continue to ruminate about emotionally upsetting events, and the higher your score on this particular scale the more you tend to do so. To put this into context, we emphasised in our original definition of stress that events in themselves are not stressful – all the event does is to provide something to ruminate about. Stress was defined as a preoccupation with emotional upset, and the rumination measure is thus a direct index of an individual's tendency to react in a stressful way to events.

The rumination measure is quite stable over time, and therefore represents a consistent, habitual way of responding. Rumination scores have also been systematically related to stress using physiological measurements such as heart-rate and blood pressure. If someone is linked to monitoring equipment and is asked to think about a distressing event, their heart-rate and blood pressure will

> if someone is asked to think about a distressing event, their **heart rate and blood pressure will increase significantly** above their resting level

increase significantly above their resting level. This happens because emotional rumination has provoked the physiological 'fight or flight' response which was described in the section on controlling attention; the hypothalamus, and in turn the inner section of the adrenal gland has been stimulated, and the level of adrenaline in the bloodstream has increased. The response may not be as intense as it was during the event itself, but is measurable and significant.

One of the consequences of this process is a rapid increase in heart-rate, in preparation for action. As we saw earlier, this is not in itself damaging – indeed, it represents an essential response to perceived threat. However, if it is sustained over a prolonged period of time, the resulting strain on the cardiovascular system is potentially damaging – and one way to sustain activation is to continue to ruminate about emotional upset after the event has passed. Emotional rumination also activates the adrenal cortex, which secretes cortisol, and as we saw earlier, prolonged high levels of cortisol can result in impairment of immune function.

Experimental studies of stress carried out in the author's laboratory have shown that the higher a person's rehearsal score, the more intense is their physiological response; and more importantly, the longer it takes them to recover afterwards. In relation to rumination, there can be little doubt that the lower the score the better. Remember, however, that having a high score does not consign you to a life of stress – it is simply a reflection of a long-standing habit, and as with all of the personality factors we shall be looking at in this section, the tendency to rehearse emotionally can be changed.

> the higher a person's rehearsal score, **the more intense is their physiological response**; and more importantly, **the longer it takes them to recover**

2. Emotional Inhibition (E-I in the appendix). The second scale included in the questionnaire you completed is emotional inhibition. As the name suggests, this measures the extent to which you bottle up emotion. It is not a measure of how emotional you are, but rather whether you bottle it up or express it. Just as with rumination, the lower the score the better. Imagine having an emotional problem that you carry around, trying to resolve it by working it over and over, but it just seems to become more and more confusing and upsetting. You then meet someone you feel able to confide in, and talking about the problem gives the feeling of a great burden having been lifted. The idea is expressed in the everyday saying of a problem shared is a problem halved, and it is the basis for the initial work in counselling. Simply being able to talk about the problem – in other words, to express the emotional feelings about it – helps to put it into perspective, and it is the expression of emotion rather than just recounting the event that is crucial.

This is the reason why expressing emotion is so important, and it goes a long way to explaining why some occupational groups appear to suffer more stress than others. In the emergency services, for example, there is often a powerful ethos that expressing emotion betrays a weakness. It is true that

> simply being able to **talk** about the problem – in other words, **to express the emotional feelings about it** – helps to put it into perspective

people in such jobs are required to inhibit emotion in some work situations, but this unfortunately becomes habitual, and they will continue to bottle up, even when there is an opportunity to acknowledge the emotion.

This example highlights two important features of emotional inhibition. The first is that it is something of a two-edged sword. In contrast to the way in which emotional rumination is one-edged – it is never useful to continue to ruminate about emotional upset – it may be necessary in some circumstances to inhibit emotion. Hence, if you have a high score on this scale, it is worth remembering that it isn't appropriate simply to vent your feeling anywhere and anytime, and knowing when and where it is appropriate requires a degree of wakefulness and attention control. Secondly, expressing emotion doesn't necessarily mean describing incidents in detail. Take the example of someone working in the emergency services, such as the police. Returning to be with partners or friends after having to deal with some particularly distressing event which demanded the inhibition of emotion does not mean that all the details have to be described, since this might only serve to distress the listener! Professional counsellors may be able to deal with this degree of disclosure since they are trained to do so, but in ordinary circumstances all that may be needed is a simple acknowledgement of being upset.

Emotional inhibition is the one scale in the pre-training questionnaire where there are significant gender differences in the average scores, with women obtaining lower scores than men. This fits in with the conventional stereotype of women being more prepared to express emotion than men, and may well be a major factor accounting for women living longer than men and suffering fewer stress-related illnesses except perhaps depression. There are other protective factors in women, including hormones that are known to confer a degree of protection against some diseases. However, large-scale analyses have suggested that, when the myriad contributory factors are taken into account, expressing emotion remains important, and it lends support to the current view that men would be better able to cope if they did express emotion more often.

Three other personality dimensions that are known to be implicated in the stress response are:

3. Toxic Achieving. The name of this dimension of personality suggests that it has an opposite, and as we shall see, there is a 'non-toxic' (or benign) aspect. In principle, the drive or motive to achieve is not in itself a problem – indeed, for anything to be done at all there has to be a desire to do it. The problem is the additional component that makes it 'toxic' or poisonous. The notion of toxic achieving was refined from an earlier index of personality called the 'Type-A Behaviour Pattern' (or simply TABP).

Type-A behaviour was characterised by a variety of features such as competitiveness, time pressure and hostility, and was developed to try to explain the incidence of heart disease amongst young men where the conventional risk factors such as smoking or obesity were absent. Unfortunately, the measures devised to measure Type-A failed to identify reliably those at risk of heart disease. This probably came about because the measures included factors that were both risky ('toxic') and neutral ('non-toxic'), and their effects may have cancelled each other out. The new toxic achieving scale was designed to distinguish between these two kinds of behaviour, where the primary risk factors are inappropriate competitiveness and anger.

> **Type-A behaviour** was characterised by a variety of features such as **competitiveness, time pressure** and **hostility**, and was developed to try to explain the incidence of **heart disease amongst young men**

For many people, changes in the nature of work over the past few decades may seem to make the feeling of time pressure, competitiveness and anger almost inevitable. As companies have shed staff ('downsized'), more work has to be done by fewer people. Nonetheless, the sense of pressure, anger and all the rest are added and unnecessary ingredients. We have constantly said in this book that it is not events that are stressful but the way in which we respond to them. We may have additional pressures, but pressure is not the same as stress. There is nothing wrong with pressure, though it is perhaps more useful to think of it as a vacuum: for most tasks there is only a limited amount of time available to do them, so there is always work still to be done. However, when this time pressure becomes a burden and is expressed as anger or hostility then it becomes toxic, and we need look no further than the physiology of fight or flight to discover why: feeling threatened or angry has the same effect as any other preoccupation with emotional upset. A significant relationship has been found between susceptibility to heart disease and this kind of behaviour, especially the anger component.

as companies have shed staff ('downsized'), **more work has to be done by fewer people.** Nonetheless, the sense of **pressure and anger** and all the rest are added and **unnecessary ingredients**

The opposite tendency is described as non-toxic achieving. This does not indicate any less desire to achieve, but there is none of the destructive, hostile form of competition. These individuals have no less to do than toxic achievers, but as always, the difference in their behaviour concerns the perception of events, not the events themselves. And more importantly, adopting a less pressured, hostile view of the world does not mean working less efficiently. Indeed, as we saw with the control of attention, being less distracted by additional preoccupations with emotional upset will allow more efficient working rather than less.

Stress is sometimes described as contagious. In principle this is untrue, but the analogy with disease is useful since you do have to be inoculated if you are to avoid catching it. In this context, inoculation means understanding that stress is an attitude of mind rather than a property of people or events, and then implementing the process of waking up and controlling attention (as we shall see shortly when we look at coping strategies, there are two further steps yet to be added). Before being inoculated, it is certainly possible to be infected by other peoples' attitudes and behaviour, and one of the consequences of toxic achieving is the effect that it has on others. What is communicated is anger and criticism, which leads in turn to

adopting a **less pressured, hostile view** of the world **does not mean working less efficiently**

one of the consequences of toxic achieving is the effect that it has on others. What is communicated is anger and criticism, which leads in turn to anger, resentment and fear

anger, resentment and fear. No organisation or team based on these principles will ever bring out the best in people, and toxic achieving is definitely a one-edged sword: the less of it the better.

4. An important feature of our behaviour is our **Desire for Control**. This is a measure of how strong a desire there is to control what happens in your life. There are many reasons for this, but it is often motivated by a fear of the unknown. There are of course things in our lives over which we can and should exercise control, and there is a strong element of choice involved here. However, the desire to control the universe is often motivated by a fear of the unknown. Many of the things that happen to us are not only beyond our control but are also unavoidable, and the appropriate way to respond to these events is to allow them to happen, preferably with a degree of emotional detachment so that the tail doesn't end up wagging the dog.

Take for example a forthcoming job interview: how often beforehand do we rehearse the event? In part, this is an appropriate process of reflecting on the kinds of questions that may be asked and what information we need to have to hand, but much of it will end up revolving around 'what if' and 'if only' scenarios. These in turn deteriorate into rumination over questions that are usually not asked and implications that may never occur, all fuelled by negative emotion and motivated by the illusion that if you can think of every possible contingency you will be in control. In the language of the Challenge of Change, these are peanuts that need to be dropped as soon as possible.

5. Sensitivity describes the ability to perceive and understand other people's emotions, and is a classic two-edged sword. Being able to perceive and respond to others' emotional feelings can be immensely beneficial, and indeed, no effective counselling could occur without it. In this context, counselling is not just a professional service rendered by appropriately trained individuals – most of us have acted as counsellors at some stage in our lives, simply by being sympathetic listeners. However, unless we can keep the emotional upset in perspective, we will ourselves become subject to it. What is needed is a detached compassion, which is not a contradiction in terms. For example, if a professional counsellor becomes identified with the problems that are being described, there will be two people with the problem, and no-one is helped. On the other hand, if the counsellor doesn't care, no-one is helped either. Hence, counselling is the practice of detached compassion.

> unless we can keep the emotional upset in perspective, **we will ourselves become subject to it**. What is needed is a **detached compassion**, which is not a contradiction in terms

It is important to remember that what is meant by detachment is not emotional coldness, and detached compassion offers not just the means for effective counselling but also a strategy for living our lives in a more fulfilling and effective way. When we are identified with our emotions rather than being detached it is impossible to respond fully to anyone else. The process of detached coping will be described in more detail in Session 6.

learning points from session 5

- Broadly speaking, we either inherit or learn the ways in which we behave. There is evidence that some aspects of our personality may be determined in part by biogenetic factors, while others appear to be more strongly influenced by learning. The most likely way in which individual differences come about is through an interaction between inherited or learned tendencies and the effects of the environment, but regardless of their origins, personality factors may be defined as **predispositions to behave in particular ways.**

- Although we may speak of personality 'types', in practice most personality factors tend to be **normally distributed in the population**. In other words, the distribution resembles a bell-shaped curve, with most people clustered about the average, and as you move towards the extremes of the distribution the fewer people there are. Consequently, it is more appropriate to speak of personality **dimensions** rather than non-overlapping types.

● The main difference between personality dimensions influenced by genetics or learning is that the former will be much more resistant to change. In relation to the personality dimensions described in this session, all of which have implications for stress, **it is perfectly possible to change.** The session described five different aspects of personality, all of which are implicated in stress to some degree: emotional rumination, emotional inhibition, toxic achieving, desire for control, and sensitivity. The first two of these are included in the sample questionnaire in the Appendix. Rumination is the most important of them, since it is a direct reflection of the tendency to become preoccupied with emotional upset and this is how stress is defined in the Challenge of Change programme. Rumination is consequently a one-edged sword, and the lower the score the better. Emotional inhibition is also implicated in stress, though it is to some extent two-edged: having a low score is preferable, but expressing emotion should take account of the context, as we saw in the example of the emergency services described in the chapter. The effects of rumination and inhibition can also usefully be seen in conjunction. If there is a high score on rumination, the effects may be mitigated to some extent if the score on inhibition is low.

> rumination is consequently a one-edged sword, and the lower the score the better. Emotional inhibition is also implicated in stress, though it is to some extent two-edged

knowing yourself: coping strategies

The personality dimensions described in the previous session represent relatively constant features of our make-up, but since they have been acquired primarily as a result of consistent reinforcement they are not indelibly fixed – they can and do change, provided some work is done to alter both behaviour and the attitudes of mind that determine behaviour.

We now turn to coping strategies, which are also highly relevant to stress. Coping strategies are usually measured by means of psychometric scales, and to a certain extent they too represent relatively stable ways of responding. We tend to have habitual, preferred strategies for dealing with situations which we perceive to be threatening or stressful.

> we tend to have **habitual**, **preferred strategies** for dealing with situations which we **perceive** to be **threatening or stressful**

However, while we do have characteristic ways of responding to stress in an attempt to cope with the conflict or agitation that it causes, a number of widely-held ideas about coping are misleading. For example, coping is often described as 'just managing to keep your head above water', but the programme described here offers a very different view: that there is no water there at all! To realise that this is so requires a fundamental change in attitude – one has to change one's mind about often strongly held beliefs.

Coping is also conventionally described in terms of three primary dimensions, labelled **rational** (or problem-focused) coping, **emotional** (or emotion-focused) coping, and **avoidance** (or denial). Traditionally, rational or problem-focused coping is seen as the opposite pole from emotional coping, but problem-focused items in coping inventories often seem to be describing how one might cope in ideal circumstances. For example, a typical problem-focused item might be finding a logical way to explain the problem, which is an unlikely strategy when someone is under stress.

An alternative is to introduce the notion of **detachment**, and recent research has shown that it is in fact detachment rather than rational coping which reflects the opposite of emotional coping. Hence, the two coping scales which will be looked at in this programme are avoidance and detachment, with the latter scale combining emotion at the one extreme and detachment at the other. These two scales differ fundamentally in being either maladaptive (avoidance) or adaptive (detached). The more important of the two is detached coping, and this is one of the three scales in the questionnaire in the appendix.

> these two scales differ fundamentally in being either **maladaptive (avoidance)** or **adaptive (detached).** The more important of the two is **detached coping**

the two coping styles

1. avoidance coping

As the name implies, avoidance might be described as the ostrich principle – burying your head in the sand and hoping it will all just go away. Because it is maladaptive, in principle, the lower the score the better – the higher the score, the more you are likely to respond to stress by just trying to avoid it. The paradox is that avoidance coping does undoubtedly work, but only in the short-term. After all, if you can effectively avoid or block something off, you don't have to attend to it, at least for the time being. This can be a

> **avoidance** might be described as **the ostrich principle** – burying your head in the sand and **hoping it will all just go away**

useful strategy. For example, faced with several tasks to do and not enough time to attend to all of them, it is appropriate to prioritise, set aside the less important ones and focus on the critical task.

However, as we all know, most things left undone don't just go away or resolve themselves – contrary to popular belief, out of sight does not mean out of mind, and unless a great deal of effort is put into ignoring them they keep on intruding. An illustration of this principle is the piece of work that keeps getting pushed to the bottom of the in-tray!

A much more dramatic illustration is the response to extreme trauma, such as post-traumatic stress. During major conflict such as the wars in Vietnam or the Falklands, soldiers and civilians were often exposed to extreme distress, and if counselling was not provided their response was sometimes to 'switch off' and try to block it all out. Initially the strategy seems to succeed, and they may appear outwardly to have adjusted, sometime for periods of ten years or more. However, if the conflict has not been resolved it may only require something relatively small to break down the barriers and flood the mind with extreme emotion. It is almost as though the trigger acts as a key which opens the door on the repository of emotion, and the consequence may be a devastating disorder requiring drug treatment or intensive therapy to resolve.

> we often respond by endlessly postponing the event, but it continues all the while to prey on our minds and distract our attention. The issue must be dealt with – all that avoidance does is to prolong the misery

Although less extreme, the use of avoidance in everyday life may have equally maladaptive consequences, despite the apparent short-term benefits. A simple illustration might be having to reprimand or confront someone about something they may have done – we often respond by endlessly postponing the event, but it continues all the while to prey on our minds and distract our attention. The issue must eventually be dealt with, and all that the avoidance does is to prolong the misery.

2. detached coping

The emotional pole of this dimension, reflected in **low scores** on the detachment component in the questionnaire, describes the tendency to become emotionally overwhelmed. This is characterised by feeling helpless, hopeless, and at the mercy of emotion, and in a sense, emotional coping might be seen as a failure to cope. We concluded earlier in this book that stress is chosen. This seems paradoxical, but the diagrams describing how attention can be captured and drawn back into the mind (see Session 3) showed why this can occur: most of our ruminative thoughts revolve around a character in the mind called 'me'.

When we suffer from stress, this becomes 'fortress me', a vulnerable individual needing to be defended against the world. This is simply a perception of ourselves, a thought; but these thoughts can change us in an instant from feeling fine to feeling worthless. All it takes is a critical comment from someone else. In fact, the only thing that has changed is an idea about 'me'. What the diagrams in Session 3 showed was that attention – the power that produces everything – is unaffected. What happens in stress is attention becomes caught, and limited to defending something small that appears to need defending.

There is an alternative choice available, and this alternative is represented by the opposite pole of the dimension, detachment. Detachment is characterised by high scores on the scale, and describes the capacity to step back from the emotion and to see things in perspective.

Learning to become detached is central to the training programme. Later in this chapter a simple strategy for beginning to free ourselves of the tyranny of negative emotion will be described in detail. However, detachment must be properly understood. Detachment is not at all like avoidance – it does not involve suppression or an attempt to deny emotion. Neither does it imply becoming cold or unemotional. One useful way of understanding detachment is by contrasting it with attachment, which is a defining feature of emotional coping – the emotion may be distressing, but you can become attached just as strongly to the negative as to the positive. This is even more clearly illus-trated with the personality dimension of rumination. You may continue to ruminate about some event and become angry or upset

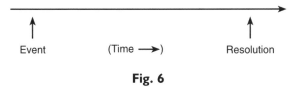

molehills remain molehills, and are not inflated into mountains

every time you do so, and even know that nothing is achieved by it, but that doesn't prevent the repetitive rumination. Clearly, there is an attach-ment to the event, and it will come as no surprise to discover that emo-tional coping and rehearsal are often closely related. By contrast, detachment means seeing things in their proper perspective – molehills remain molehills, and are not inflated into mountains. And once there is detachment, there is the opportunity to let go of the negative emotion.

Detachment provides the real meaning of the parable of the monkey and the peanut described in the section on controlling attention, where the monkey puts his hand through the hole in the pot and is caught because he won't let the peanut go. The forest is full of food, but because of attachment he is unable to put it into perspective; he gives up his life for a peanut.

The idea of detachment and letting go needs to put into a wider per-spective, and this can be done using the timeline shown below.

Event   (Time ⟶)   Resolution

Fig. 6

Towards the left hand end of the line is a point marking a distressing event – having had an argument with someone, or our earlier example of hurrying to a meeting and becoming stuck in a traffic queue. The stressful (and commonplace) response is to continue to ruminate about it, so that thoughts about the event keep intruding in the mind. Later that same day and perhaps for days or weeks afterwards, the event comes to mind again and again. At some point, however, it comes to mind once more, but this time you are able to detach yourself from it, and to stop the mechanical cycle of emotional upset. You might even say to yourself that the whole affair was trivial and not worth getting upset about. This is the point of

resolution shown on the right-hand side of the timeline, and the aim of stress management is to bring the point of resolution as close to the event as possible.

In the case of the everyday events we've been using as illustrations, this need not take more than a matter of seconds, but two points are worth remembering. Firstly, the 'window of opportunity' in which you can take action may be very short, so if it is not taken within that time, the likelihood is that you will simply be caught once again. Secondly, in order to avail yourself of that opportunity you must be awake – it goes without saying that in waking sleep there is no opportunity to control attention and detach, and to miss the opportunity is to sacrifice one's life for peanuts.

the **window of opportunity** in which you can take action may be **very short**, so if it is not taken within that time, the likelihood is that you will simply be **caught again**

We saw at the start of this book that there is in principle no such thing as a stressful event, and that remains true. So how are we to respond to less commonplace events, such as the death of someone close to us? Few people would claim to be able to resolve them in seconds, and in these cases most people would suffer grief. This is quite natural, and it would be inappropriate to respond by saying 'so what, everyone dies'.

However, it is equally inappropriate to go on grieving for the rest of your life: at some point, there is resolution or acceptance that everyone does indeed die. That point on the timeline may be well to the right, and it may take months or even years to come to terms with grief. No-one else can dictate how long it 'should' take, but eventually resolution must come if we are to go on living our lives.

In the case of bereavement, counselling often helps people to move towards resolution, partly because the grieving person is able to express and let go of their emotions but also because the counsellor offers a detached 'third point' from which to view the situation with greater objectivity. Counselling provides a useful analogy for understanding detachment. If a counsellor identifies with all the distress being expressed, then he or she also becomes distressed and no-one is helped. At the other extreme, if the counsellor doesn't care about the client's distress, no-one is helped either. Counselling demands **detached compassion**, which as we said earlier is not a contradiction in terms – because detachment does not mean coldness, it is perfectly possible to be both detached and compassionate at the same time. Detached compassion offers a way not only to counsel others, but to counsel oneself – it offers a way of living one's life without stress.

detachment and the 'three houses'

A simple illustration of the different ways of coping makes use of an analogy in which the mind is represented as a house. This is shown in the diagram below, where the house is represented as having two doors and with a flood to the one side of the house only (remember, it is only an analogy!):

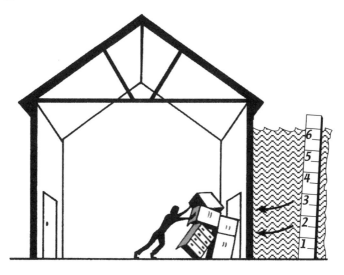

Fig. 7

The flood represents all of our emotional experiences stored up in memory, as well as what we anticipate in the future. For example, if you are asked to think back to what you had for lunch yesterday, if you can remember it is recalled from the flood. In our analogy, it has been brought in through the door, and you can only be aware of something consciously when it is inside the 'house' of the mind.

Extending the analogy to stress, as we well know, negative or distressing emotions keep intruding into our minds; it is as if there is pressure from the flood outside the door, which keeps breaking in. One way of responding to this pressure is, by analogy, to pile the furniture up against the door, and this represents avoidance coping. Avoiding or ignoring things will have a short-term benefit, but the pressure remains and may eventually break the door down and overwhelm you, as the next diagram shows:

Fig. 8

This happens most dramatically in post-traumatic stress, but whether it is day-to-day stress or major trauma, the effect is the same: we become absorbed in the thought, and the thought is just a dream (or in the case of stress, a nightmare). Just as with dreams in dreaming sleep, the events we ruminate about in waking sleep are re-lived and seem real at the time – only when we wake up do we recognise it as only a dream. Unfortunately, by then we have already been caught, and simply trying to avoid things by blocking them from the mind cannot be sustained.

Not everyone uses avoidance to the same degree. What is far more typical of our reactions to distress is that the door to the right of the house, holding back the flood, is more like the saloon door in a Western movie – it just swings open under pressure. For example, we have an argument, and for the next few days the whole incident keeps coming back into the mind from memory, as if from nowhere. The consequence is the same: once the flood breaks in, you're overwhelmed and end up drowning in the flood. The reaction may not be as intense as the argu-ment itself was, but when the emotion takes hold it appears to fill your whole experience. This is the equivalent of emotional 'coping', which as we have said represents more of a failure to cope.

What is the alternative? The first point to remember is that the flood is not going to go away. We all experience emotion, some of it negative, and there is nothing unnatural about that. What is unnatural is to try to deny it, and stress management is not about searching around at the bot-tom of the flood for the plug so it can all be drained away. By the same token, if you shut this door and try to keep it shut, the pressure will sim-ply grow until eventually the door breaks down and the flood pours in.

However, the second point is to realise that our house of the mind has, as it were, a 'loft'. When we are able to put things into perspective, it is as if we have stepped back from them – by analogy, we go up into the loft. This is not denying or trying to avoid them – we acknowledge them, but are no longer overwhelmed by them. This perspective is taken from what we are calling the loft in the house, a position which is detached and not overwhelmed.

Putting these two points together, the way to deal with the pressure is to open the door at the far end of the house from the flood, and then open the door where the flood is. Then, keeping them open, you run upstairs into the loft and let it all flow through below you! This is shown in the diagram below.

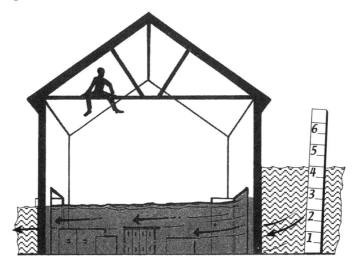

Fig. 9

If this seems simplistic, it can very easily be illustrated. Suppose you bring to mind something that upset you recently. If you continue to ruminate about it, the distressing thought will eventually fill the mind to the exclusion of everything else. Your attention will have been completely absorbed.

You can then take the simple step of being aware or observing the distressing thoughts in your mind. It is quite a simple move from being identified with thoughts or ideas in the mind to observing or being aware of them. Once the thought is under observation and you are no longer identified with it, and you are, in our analogy, in the loft.

Next, take control of your attention and give it fully to something else – listen to the sounds you can hear outside, for example. Once you do so, what happens to the idea that a moment ago was filling the mind? It has disappeared, which in our analogy means that it has passed out of the other door. By connecting your attention with your senses, you came back into the present – literally, you come to your senses.

However, as we know, the thoughts don't just disappear for ever; they have a nasty habit of circling straight back round again – repetitious, intrusive thoughts are just that! What this shows is that you can't obliterate emotional memories, any more than you can go on denying them indefinitely. All that you can do is to step back from them and to practise waking up, controlling attention and becoming detached. The more you identify with negative emotion the more strength you give it. You can acknowledge it but remain detached, and even though it may still keep coming back, it will do so with less and less power to overwhelm the mind. And once you've taken the first three steps of waking up, controlling attention and becoming detached, you can then let go the negative emotion and allow reason to prevail.

> once you've taken the first three steps of **waking up, controlling attention and becoming detached**, you can then let go the negative emotion and **allow reason to prevail**

When arguing with someone, we often think or even say, 'just be reasonable'. What we are asking for is freedom from the tyranny of negative emotion, in this case anger, so that reason can return. Then the dog can begin to wag the tail, rather than the tail wag the dog.

becoming free the gentle way

One of the opinions commonly expressed by people who have heard this training programme is that it accords with their own common sense, and is therefore something they can easily envisage putting into practice. Encouraging though this may be, it brings with it the danger of expectation – no sooner has the programme been heard than people find themselves falling back into the old habitual ways of responding.

In fact, this should not surprise anyone. We have been conditioned for most of our lives to behave in ways which are maladaptive, such as identification rather than detachment, and old habits die hard. Unfortunately, we're also conditioned to expect instant results, and it may be useful to keep in mind the analogy of learning to ride a bicycle. Our first response is to jump on and have a go, and promptly fall off. Instruction may help in pointing the way, but ultimately it is practice alone that will lead to expertise.

So also with this programme. The course itself helps to show what stress is really about, to show the reasons why we end up suffering from stress and to indicate ways in which our attitudes and the behaviour they support can change, but change itself depends upon persistent practice. If we appear to stumble at the first hurdle, we may move from the correct judgement, that this is easier said than done, to the incorrect one, that this is too difficult to do. Hence the need to be uncritical of your own apparent failures, and simply to put behind you having been caught again by anger or upset. After all, to know you had been caught again you have to have woken up from it, and the first big step – being aware of it – has already been taken.

From then on, what people typically experience is a growing frequency of waking up, even though at first it may be after the event. Then there is waking up in the midst of it all, for example discovering how much one's mind has been taken over by anger in the heat of an argument, and being able to see it for what it is and change the whole direction of the conversation. This leads in turn to a growing number of occasions when the inoculation works as it should, and the window of opportunity opens up before the event has even occurred – coming across the traffic jam, and knowing that no amount of anger will have any effect except to give you a short, miserable life.

if
all this **habitual**
behaviour is so damaging, **why**
do people do it – where does it
come from? And **what keeps**
it in place?

One question which often arises is why, if all this habitual behaviour is so damaging, do people do it – where does it come from? And what keeps it in place? The first question we have already tackled to some extent when we looked at personality, and we concluded that those aspects of personality which are implicated in stress appear largely to have been learned through the process of socialisation. This is probably partly a cultural issue, and Western organisational culture undoubtedly encourages a lot of the time-pressured and over-identified ways in which we work.

However, we are not subject to these influences entirely, and we can take what is good and useful from them and leave the rest. After all, most of us know people who are far more easy-going than we are about these pressures, but without becoming unproductive or not caring – it is simply a matter of what you attach importance to. The message of this programme is that working well and efficiently is important; becoming stressed by it all (in other words, worrying about things you can do nothing about) is not.

The second question is an interesting one – what keeps it all in place? One aspect of our personality which is particularly difficult to measure is self-esteem, but it is perhaps the most important one of all. Toxic achievers often take on the toxic anger and time pressure as a way of compensation for a fear of possible failure, or doubt about themselves. In the same way, rumination, emotional inhibition and all the other behaviours we've described ultimately circle around the character we described earlier in this chapter as 'me', and to whom almost everything we do is dedicated. If your feeling about this 'me' is like a fortress that has to be defended day and night, with the troops on the battlements armed to the teeth, that must lead to exhaustion.

The key is to realise the fortress is empty, in the sense that provided you acknowledge both your strengths and limitation, there is nothing that needs defending. This programme is as much one of training in empowerment as anything else, giving people back the power they've always had but which bad habits have covered over with uncertainty, defensiveness and negative emotion. The feeling of helplessness which characterises stress can begin to be overcome by remembering that there is one thing you always have complete control over: your own attention. It is the power that produces the greatest achievements we know of, and everyone has it to the same degree. Our talents may differ, but attention is the same, and you can give attention to what you choose.

the feeling of **helplessness** which characterises stress can begin to be overcome by remembering that there is one thing you always have **complete control** over: **your own attention**

To summarise the last two sessions, what we have looked at are those aspects of our personality and our habitual ways of coping which might serve either to make us more vulnerable to, or protect us from, stress. In the process we have added a third step to the original sequence of waking up, controlling attention and letting go: **becoming detached**. To do so we used the analogy of the mind as a house with two doors, and with a flood at the one side of the house behind the door. The important point here was that the flood of emotion is not of itself unnatural, and stress management is certainly not about becoming unemotional. Instead, we proposed that the house of the mind has a 'loft', the vantage point from which we can get things into perspective. To go into the loft does not mean to withdraw, it is simply stepping back and seeing things for what they are, without becoming overwhelmed. From this vantage point we can let go – allow the intrusive distress to flow straight through the mind, without identifying with it. This does not mean it disappears, and the four-fold process of waking up, controlling attention, becoming detached and letting go will work only for as long as it is practised.

learning points from session 6

- Coping styles may be **maladaptive** or **adaptive**. Maladaptive styles have the effect of making us more vulnerable while adaptive styles help us to deal with demands.
- The maladaptive style illustrated in this section was **avoidance** – the habit of denying things, in the hope that they will just go away. As we saw this has short-term benefits only, since in the long run the pressure of the denied emotion will burst open the door to the mind.

- The long-term effect of denial is becoming **overwhelmed by negative emotion**, which will also happen if there is no attempt to control attention, as in the second example of the house of the mind.
- The alternative is to use the adaptive strategy of **detachment**, though it must be remembered that this does not mean emotional coldness – the analogy that is used is from counselling, which requires **detached compassion**.

communication, stress and effective management

You may be wondering why a session on communication has been included in a programme on stress management. Stress is certainly the central theme, but by defining stress in the way we have done, as a preoccupation with emotional upset, it follows that stress is likely to lead to poor communication. Poor communication will in turn lead to stress, creating a cycle that compromises teamwork and impairs performance.

For example, if a new management system is being introduced into your company but is not communicated properly, the consequence is uncertainty, anxiety, ill-feeling and even anger, all of which are ruminated about without resolution. For the individual, this means misery at work; for the company it could mean the difference between thriving and either limping along or failing altogether.

In the author's experience, training in 'soft' skills such as human relations, communication and stress management are particularly vulnerable to cutbacks in times of budgetary restraint. This is a short-sighted policy, since for the most part, the real heart of a company is not its plant and machinery but its people. There appears to be a widespread assumption amongst many managers that people don't want to work, and that managing them means finding ways of coercing them to do so. Few managers have learnt how to create

> if a **new management system** is being introduced into your company but is not **communicated** properly, the consequence is uncertainty, anxiety, ill-feeling and even **anger**

a **different view** is to see **people** as an **untapped source of tremendous talent,** powered by attention, and to regard the role of management as ensuring that **this talent is released** for the benefit of both the employees and the **company**

long-term trusting and supportive relationships that enable people to develop and exploit their talents, and in these circumstances, job satisfaction is bound to be low. A different view is to see people as an untapped source of tremendous talent, powered by attention, and to regard the role of management as ensuring that this talent is released for the benefit of both the employees and the company.

skilled communication

Given this background, stress and communication are inextricably linked. As with stress management we shall start by asking how communication skills training is usually approached. The figure below represents a conventional communication skills model.

what communication skills training is usually about: a communications 'tool kit'

R   **recognition** of the other person
E   **eye contact**, showing a willingness to engage
L   **listening**, showing continued interest and attention
A   **attitudes** which might hinder communication
T   **turn-taking**, showing the exchange is reciprocal
E   **expression**, showing that what is said is what is felt

Down the left hand side of the diagram is the acronym RELATE, with each letter referring to a particular aspect of communication skill. This is often described as a communications 'tool kit' because communication skills are regarded as a set of tools that are used according to the demands of the situation. These tools have certain rules for their use, just as in any tool kit: screwdrivers are used differently from hammers. In communication, one of the best-known aspects is eye-contact, and it is assumed that in order to communicate effectively you have to maintain eye contact for a certain proportion of time during conversation. This is illustrated by trying to communicate with someone who is either constantly fixing you with a stare, or alternatively never meets your gaze – both of these patterns tend to make communication difficult.

At the same time, it is hard to generate a rule about the right amount of eye contact. You might decide that gaze should be maintained 50% of the time, and proceed to train someone lacking in communication skills to do so. In all probability, he or she will then dutifully apply the rule but still find that communication is unsatisfactory. The reason is that there is no inflexible rule that can be applied, and indeed, compared with one another, skilled communicators may use very different gaze patterns, and may vary the amount of eye-contact they engage in during the course of a conversation. Skilled communication is more a case of responding to what is needed in the situation rather than the simple application of a rule.

The same is true of turn-taking, the 'T' in the RELATE model. Turn-taking describes the reciprocal nature of conversation, and there is a whole pattern of gestures, intonation and grammar which mark the points when the speaker is prepared to relinquish the turn and allow the other person to speak. In formal discourse these points tend to be fairly clearly demarcated, but when conversation becomes animated the turn may be exchanged very quickly indeed, and will render the application of rules learned by rote impossible.

This is not to say that appropriate eye contact and turn-taking are unimportant for communication – clearly they are. What is not appropriate is the attempt to use an inflexible 'rules and tools' approach, and the principle applies equally to the other components of the RELATE acronym. For example, we clearly need to listen if we are to communicate at all, and as a rule a conversation consists of one person speaking and another listening.

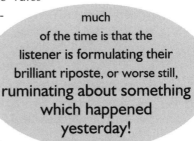

much of the time is that the listener is formulating their brilliant riposte, or worse still, **ruminating about something which happened yesterday!**

Unfortunately, what is actually happening much of the time is that the listener is formulating their brilliant riposte, or worse still, ruminating about something which happened yesterday! When this occurs attention is being given to something else rather than the speaker, and communication has effectively ceased; little wonder that we so often feel misunderstood, or fail to understand anyone else.

Attitudes are also important, and we've made reference to them before. Some people are described as having an 'attitude problem', but it is attitudes themselves that are the problem. Take the example of walking into a room for the first time: at that point you will generally be alert and attending because of the novelty. However, the next time you walk into the room, you have an expectation of what you will find. In a sense you don't walk into the room at all, you simply walk into an expectation, an idea held in the mind and dictated by the past. This is equally true of people we 'know' – after the first meeting, what we know is an idea about that person arrived at as a construction in the mind, an attitude. This is the basis of **prejudice**, since most of our views about others are pre-judgements based on a first encounter in the past. Consequently, attitudes can hinder not only communication but every other way we conduct our lives as well.

what we know is an **idea about that person** arrived at as a construction in the mind, an attitude. **This is the basis of prejudice**

In fact, everything we're exposed to passes through a screen of attitudes, and becomes personalised and coloured by our views. Much of what we call 'my life' is distorted recollection, with little objective reality.

The difficulty of applying rules and tools may seem to make the whole process of communication altogether too problematic, but if you want to communicate effectively, there is one fundamental principle: **you have to be awake.** The first step is no different from stress management, and neither is the second step of controlling attention. We can look again at our diagram describing the continuum from deep sleep to wide awake which we used in the context of managing stress, and ask the question 'when can we communicate'?

WIDE AWAKE
Only in this state can we respond to
who is there and what is actually being said.

|

WAKING SLEEP
In waking sleep there is the appearance of
communication, but where is our attention?

|

SLEEPWALKING
A sleepwalker may react to directions,
but again this is hardly communication.

|

DREAMING SLEEP
In dreaming sleep the dreamer may
talk, but this is hardly communication.

|

DEEP SLEEP
In deep sleep there is clearly no communication.

Fig. 10.

As the diagram shows, in deep sleep there is plainly no communication at all. In dreaming sleep, the dreamer may well respond in a fashion to your questions, but that can hardly be called communication. The same is true of the next stage, sleep walking – if the person is told to go back to bed they may well do so, but this is hardly communication. In the stage we called 'waking sleep', outward attention to what is happening in the present has been snatched away. There may be every appearance of communication, but attention is distracted by ideas from the past or future.

Only when we are wide awake can we can really respond to who is there and what is being said. The next figure shows a simple contrast between communicating while awake in the left-hand column and communicating while asleep in the right-hand column:

AWAKE	ASLEEP
(i) Communication is **spontaneous**, responsive to the here-and-now.	Communication is based on **fixed ideas** from the past.
(ii) Attention is **controlled** and focused outwards on the other.	Attention control is **lost**, focused inwards on 'me'.
(iii) There is **co-operation** for the speaking turn.	There is **competition** for the speaking turn.
(iv) There is **tolerance** of others.	There is **criticism** of others.
(v) People are **separated** from their work and roles.	People are **confused** with their work and roles.

Fig. 11.

Taking each of these steps in turn, first of all, when you are awake communication is **spontaneous**. This doesn't mean doing things on the spur of the moment, without thought. The dictionary defines spontaneous as an unforced, natural process, and for our purposes the word spontaneous means being in the present, responding to what is here and now. In the 'asleep' column things are quite the opposite – communication is based on ideas from the past or the future.

The second step asks what has happened to our **attention**. As we saw earlier, being awake means that attention is controlled and focused outwards on the event taking place at the time, and in the case of communication that event is the person you are communicating with. When in waking sleep, attention control is lost, focused inwards on this character that we described as 'me', or on some event or emotion from the past or future.

In the third step, when we are awake there is **co-operation**, with listeners listening when they are supposed to be. When we are asleep there is competition for the floor, or listeners not listening but merely formulating what they think is their brilliant reply.

In the fourth step this leads to intolerance as you desperately try to get your bit said, and to criticism and argument. When we are awake, we are much more likely to be tolerant.

In the final step, when we are awake we can **separate people from their roles**, whereas asleep, people are confused with their roles. Together with the negative effect of criticism, this is the most important aspect of communication, and we shall be expanding on them in the next session.

communication, management and stress

A useful distinction can be drawn between two types of leadership: ascribed and achieved. **Ascribed leadership** is a function of the particular rank you have, which in a military context might be shown by a badge, or in a company by a title. These badges and the like are symbols of rank, and they confer authority irrespective of the individual wearing them – you may dislike the person, but you have no choice other than to obey. In contrast to this is **achieved leadership**, where people are followed because they are respected, and have earned the role.

> **what kinds of companies** are based on **respect** rather than **fear?** One way of looking at it is to think about managers and organisations that are either **awake or asleep**

So what kind of person earns a leadership role? What kinds of companies are based on respect rather than fear? One way of looking at it is to think about managers and organisations that are either awake or asleep. Those that are awake:

● Evaluate the work, not the person.
● Acknowledge a job well done.
● Regard problems are 'ours', not 'yours'.
● Pull together under pressure.
● Are inspiring, tolerant and decisive.

In these organisations, there is **mutual** respect both upwards and downwards. They have an inspiring, tolerant and decisive ethos, and they are a pleasure to work for.

By contrast, managers whose position has merely been ascribed and not earned may not have the respect and co-operation of their staff, and may then have to impose their

> criticism is often justified as 'constructive criticism', but **there is no such thing as constructive criticism**

authority by resorting to management by threat. These mis-managers hardly manage at all, they simply have titles, and in terms of our definitions are asleep. They tend to rule by criticism, which is always destructive.

Criticism is often justified as 'constructive criticism', but there is no such thing as constructive criticism. To criticise is to take apart and to construct is to put together, so they can't be done at the same time. All that criticism does is to destroy people's self-esteem and any loyalty they might have had. Managers who operate in sleep criticise people rather than work, they don't acknowledge excellence, they pass the buck when things go wrong and their teams disintegrate under pressure. Management is then based around fear, anger and demand; when times are difficult there is naming, blaming and shaming of those above and below. Working for these companies ends up feeling like a life sentence.

In addition to criticism, the most important feature which distinguishes between good and bad management is whether or not the person and the role are separated. To understand what this means requires an important principle: don't take work seriously! A common response to this statement is to misinterpret it as not caring, because as a rule we tend to 'think in twos'. The idea of not taking work seriously then brings two pictures to mind: in one, there is someone racing about desperately trying to get everything done yesterday, and in the other is someone with their feet up on the table. In fact, neither is appropriate. Desperation leads to an unhappy life, but putting your feet up means doing nothing and probably losing your job. What is important is finding a third way that balances these two out. This is not simply finding some halfway point between the two. It is quite a different view, and just as with stress management, involves becoming detached. However, in this context, it means becoming detached from work.

> desperation leads to an **unhappy life**, but putting your feet up means doing nothing and probably **losing your job**. What is important is finding a **third way** that balances these two out

It is widely recognised that so-called constructive criticism leads to dissatisfaction and low self-esteem, and as an alternative it was proposed that managers should give feedback. Unfortunately, however, feedback has never been clearly operationalised, and people attempting to use it often slip into criticism. What is required is an identifiable procedure, and the Challenge of Change system offers a staged process for effective communication. This starts with the first principles of waking up and controlling attention – in other words, being in the present and aware, and free from the prejudices carried in our attitudes. The next step involves detaching people from their roles, which in a work context means their job. A job is not you, it is simply one of the many roles that you perform.

For example, if you ask someone who they are and they give you a job title, then when they retire they no longer exist! This is a consequence of attachment or identification with work. When this happens we effectively **become** our work, and anything said about the work I do is, by implication, also said about me. This is shown clearly in the diagram below.

Fig. 12

On the one side is you, on the other side is me and my work. As far as I'm concerned I **am** my work, so in this case when anything is said about the work it is also said about me: both me and the work become the target. On the other hand, we can be **detached** from work, so that what I do is a role I perform and you and I can objectively evaluate whether or not it has reached the required standard:

Fig. 13

Here the work is the target, which is entirely legitimate. There is a standard for every job, and it our task is to do it as well as we can. If it doesn't achieve the standard, then together we can decide what needs to be done in order to bring that about. People are never legitimate targets, and in our own experience, when we take comments about our work personally, the effect is anger, resentment and fear. One simple management principle is that everyone in the company has a multitude of talents and skills, and good management is about allowing these talents and skills to flourish naturally for the benefit of that individual as well as the company.

This is what is meant by not taking work seriously – it means not thinking that you are your job. In fact, only when you are detached from a job can you do it properly. Without detachment comes the 'parallel processing': concern about doing it well enough, and worry about the consequences of it being done wrong. In other words, rumination, which divides attention between the work and the worry about the work.

Which is not to say that you don't care about doing it well – on the contrary, as with stress management, what is let go is the negative emotion, not the work, and that frees your attention for the work alone. More importantly, it means that comments made about our work are not taken as judgements of us as individuals. After all, most of us are capable of judging the standard of many kinds of work; who among us is able to judge the standard of a person? This is not an argument for sacrificing standards, but rather that it is work, not people, which must reach that standard.

In the real world, work is often not done perfectly for all kinds of reasons – there may not be enough time or enough people, or the people doing the work may not have the skills and need more training. But this is not a comment on the person – skills are the ways that people do things, and can be improved in the same way that one can acquire a better tool to do a particular job. All that has improved is the tool; people are trained to improve their skills, not themselves.

One of the problems in communication is that it is a very subtle process, and we often take for granted that others have understood us, or we feel obliged to indicate that we understand, even when we may not have done so. With communication, it is safest not to take anything for granted. You might even go to the extent of actually drawing these little diagrams when someone brings work to you, showing the two of you on the one side and the work on the other.

In conclusion, in order to communicate we have to wake up, control attention, detach the person from the work, and let go of the negative emotion that pressure brings with it. The process is no different from managing stress: we can only communicate when we're awake, we can only hear what is being said if we give attention, we can only be free from taking personally things said about our work by being detached. Unless we let go there will be conflict. The steps are simple; all that is required is practice at changing our habitual ways of thinking and acting.

learning points from session 7

- Acquiring good communication skills is not about learning **'rules and tools'** of communication – the process is extremely subtle, and cannot be learnt by rote.
- In fact, as with stress management, the first step in the process is to **wake up, followed by controlling attention** so that it focuses on the person we're communicating with.
- **There is no such thing as 'constructive criticism',** and criticism and the feelings of low self-esteem which follow from criticism require the final step of detachment.
- In the context of communication, detachment means **separating the person from the work they do or the role they perform**. In this way, the work can be evaluated without taking the comments personally. Work must be done to a standard, but it is the work and not the person that needs to reach that standard – people are not legitimate targets.

session

8

relaxation

When we looked at what stress management is usually about, we noted that one of the features of conventional stress management is relaxation. We said at the time that relaxation tends to deal primarily with the body, and to that extent its effects are likely to be palliative, since the body is, in a sense, a symptom of the mind. What runs in the mind is reflected in the body, and tension in the body is generated in part by activity in the mind.

> relaxation tends to deal primarily with the body, and to that extent its effects are likely to be palliative, since the body is, in a sense, a symptom of the mind

However, we also said that relaxation, although palliative, is useful. This is particularly true if you can also relax your mind. Here are three simple exercises in relaxing the body and the mind (relaxation of the body is further divided into deep and rapid relaxation techniques).

deep relaxation

In order to relax we have first to find a comfortable position for the body. With deep relaxation that usually means lying down, though not necessarily – it is perfectly possible to relax sitting in a chair. Paradoxically, however, relaxing in a chair is easier the more upright your posture. As your body slides down in a chair, your spine curves and it becomes more difficult to breathe easily. The

paradoxically, **relaxing in a chair is easier the more upright your posture**. As your body slides down in a chair, your spine curves and it becomes **more difficult to breathe**

ideal chair is firm and with an upright backrest. You should also have your feet flat on the floor, since crossing your legs impedes the circulation of the blood and will quickly lead to discomfort.

As with all of the techniques described in the book, controlling attention is all-important, so having found a comfortable position, either lying on your back or in a supportive chair, begin by giving your attention to your breathing. Relax all of the muscles in your chest and stomach, and take a deep breath to start with, if you need to. Then, relaxing all of the muscles in chest and stomach, just allow the breath to come and go naturally. Don't try to breathe more deeply or more shallowly, but make sure that both chest and stomach rise and fall with each breath.

Once the breathing is relaxed and regular, give your attention to the first 'gate' in the body, where your neck and shoulders meet. A great deal of tension builds up here during the course of the day, and is the source of many tension headaches (indeed, one of the first benefits of learning to relax is a reduction in tension headaches). Now relax your shoulders, and with your arms and head balanced and relaxed if you're sitting up, or supported lying down, allow that relaxation to extend all the way down your arms to your hands. When this gate is shut by tension, the circulation of the blood is inhibited, so as you relax be aware of the circulation of the blood beginning to flow freely all the way down to your fingers. Then give your attention to your neck, your scalp and your face, letting all tension go from around your eyes, your mouth and your jaw. Very simply, with each **out breath**, allow the last remaining tension to dissolve from the first gate.

Next give your attention to the second 'gate', which is in your pelvis. The tension here is holding in and tightening all of the muscles in the pelvis. Let all of that tension go, and as you do so, relax all of the muscles in your thighs, calves and feet. If you're sitting, be aware of the weight of your feet on the floor. Then be aware of the circulation flowing freely all the way down to your toes, and with each out breath, allow the last remaining tension to dissolve from this second gate in the pelvis.

Then be aware of your body as a whole, which is now completely supported, with no effort at all, and with each out breath release any remaining tension in the body.

rapid relaxation

Learning to relax in this way is very important, but you may well go to sleep doing so! This will be a deep, relaxing sleep, and very beneficial, partly because it is progressive and keeps your attention controlled all the way to sleep. This means that attention is taken away from the ruminative thoughts that are the source of tension.

having learnt to relax **you can't go off for an hour or so to relax while at work.** For this reason, **a rapid technique** is also required

However, having learnt to relax you can't go off for an hour or so to relax while at work. For this reason, a rapid technique is also required. This begins by literally stopping whatever you are doing, so there must be an appropriate opportunity for it. Having stopped, this is followed immediately by firstly checking the body for any tension, then simply letting all the tension drop away. Once you know from deep relaxation what you're aiming for, the process can be completed in a matter of seconds, and you can then return to the task in hand. Three simple steps: Stop, Check, Let go.

relaxing the mind

Unfortunately, if you stop and check again five minutes later the tension may well have returned, since it is being generated by activity in both the body and the mind. Finding that the tension has returned does not negate the practice – there are substantial benefits to be gained from relaxing as often as possible, even if the effects are not permanent – but the greater benefits come with the next step of relaxing the mind.

To relax the mind is not to 'switch off'. After all, the mind is never actually switched off; all that happens is that you give attention to something else. To relax the mind you need to have **presence of mind**, in order to relax the mind is not to 'switch off'. After all, the mind is never actually switched off; all that happens is that you give attention to something else to let go of all of the pre-occupations with yesterday and tomorrow which drain away your energy.

This is achieved by connecting with your senses, and is most easily illustrated by listening. Whenever you remember, stop whatever you are doing, briefly close your eyes and listen. Try to keep your attention on whatever you can hear in each moment, without allowing pictures and associations to form, and by returning to listening each time you find that your attention has been taken by some idea about the past or the future. In this way, with presence of mind, all concerns fall away, and can then be seen in their proper perspective.

The techniques for the deep and rapid relaxation of the body and the relaxation of the mind described here may be summarised as follows:

relaxing the body: deep

1. Opening the first gate (neck and shoulders).
2. Opening the second gate (pelvis).
3. Freeing circulation.
4. Letting go with out breaths.

relaxing the body: rapid

1. 'Stopping'.
2. Relaxing by checking and loosening.

relaxing the mind

1. 'Stopping'.
2. Freeing outward attention.
3. Changing time perspective (having 'presence of mind').

relaxation, hypnosis and meditation

These exercises are practiced briefly during the course of the Challenge of Change training days, and participants often ask whether this is hypnosis or meditation. None of the exercises have anything in common with hypnosis, which in some ways can be seen as someone else (the hypnotist) taking control of your attention. The training emphasises the opposite, and is based on empowering people to take control of their own attention.

There is, however, a relationship with meditation, especially the exercise of relaxing the mind. Much has been written about meditation, usually in a spiritual or philosophical context. Amongst Westerners, it is also commonly associated with Eastern philosophy, a view that was reinforced when celebrities like the Beatles became involved in the transcendental meditation movement. The techniques vary but typically involve the repetition in the mind of a word, called a mantra. A mantra is thought to have spiritual significance, and to be directly instrumental in bringing about the peace of mind that meditation offers.

There has been a substantial amount of research on the effects of meditation, and there is little doubt that it can lead to a calmer, more stress-free state of mind. There is also very good evidence that regular meditation can help to reduce stress-related conditions such as high blood pressure. However, meditation need not necessarily be invested with the mystique of spirituality. An alternative view is that it represents an exercise in attention control, with the attention constantly brought back to the word being repeated in the mind. Gradually, without the support of attention, the other preoccupations in the mind become less and less important, and can be seen more easily for what they are – just thoughts. In this view, any word will work. For example, you could repeat a word like 'one', but bear in mind that some words may conjure up particular associations in the mind and lead to ruminating about them!

> **meditation** need not necessarily be invested with the **mystique of spirituality.** An alternative view is that it represents **an exercise in attention control**

The link with rumination and attention becomes clear when people first start to try meditation – very soon, attention is drawn back to yesterday and tomorrow. To succeed requires persistent and regular practice. A starting point is the exercise of relaxing the mind described in this chapter. Just listening, without making any judgements about what you can hear, is a kind of outward meditation, whereas repeating a word in the mind turns the attention inwards. The effect is similar – the mind becomes awake but still, and the practice can gradually be extended from a few minutes to perhaps 20 or 30 minutes twice daily. For most of us, conditioned as we are to value rushing around trying to get everything under control, the idea of doing nothing seems strange, but even a small amount of practice can provide significant benefits.

stress management in perspective

To summarise what has been described in this book, the training programme begins with the assumption that everything changes, and that change cannot be avoided. Paradoxically, while we enjoy change and novelty, we also suffer the stress that comes from not being able to adapt successfully when it occurs. Change is consequently a challenge, and to able to respond appropriately we need to have a clear understanding of what stress is.

The programme distinguishes between post-traumatic stress and day-to-day stress. Post-traumatic stress is a response to an overload of emotional demand, and is a diagnosable disorder that may require a range of treatment strate-gies to help overcome it. However, traumatic events are fortunately relatively rare, and the emphasis in the book is instead on day-to-day stress. The tech-niques described here are based on a preventative approach, and are aimed at inoculation against stress.

> while we enjoy change and novelty, we also suffer the stress that comes from not being able to adapt successfully when it occurs. Change is consequently a challenge

The Challenge of Change programme differs markedly from conventional stress management training, which tends to be based on symptoms of stress, life events and relaxation. The symptoms of day-to-day stress can too easily be concealed to allow a reliable diagnosis, and people differ widely in their thresholds for feeling stressed – for some, just one symptom would suffice, while others seem able to tolerate a great deal more. Unlike post-traumatic stress, everyday stress can seldom be identified with confidence.

The most important limitation of using life events to describe stress is that they attribute a 'stress quotient' to almost everything that might happen to you. In fact, stress is how we respond to the event, not the event itself. If this were not the case there would be no stress management – few events can be avoided, and all that life events do is to provide the themes that people ruminate about. Relaxation is a useful strategy, but is of limited use unless it extends to relaxing the mind as well as the body.

By contrast, the Challenge of Change programme argues that people tend to be asleep much of the time, with their attention snatched back into the mind where it recycles distorted memories from the past or anticipated events in the future. Since this is all fantasy, it is merely a dream, and when it is coloured by negative emotion it turns into the nightmare of stress. Stress can helpfully be defined as ruminating about emotional upset, a 'what if?' and 'if-only' worry that has no effect on the problem in hand. This is not the same as intentionally giving attention to something. Making plans and drawing on experience in a rational way is entirely appropriate, but this is quite different from having your attention snatched away.

A simple model of the way mind operates is to think of events as providing information (the input), the mind or brain processing the information, and then giving output in the form of attention. Attention is the power that produces everything that we create, from the mundane to the sublime, but nothing is produced when attention is captured and drawn back into the mind where it circles round on the current re-play. All of the actual action takes place in the here-and-now, hence the description of someone acting absolutely appropriately having 'presence of mind'. There is a simple way to come into the present, and that is to connect attention to the senses. The senses only work in the present, and again there is a phrase that captures it – on seeing things for what they are, we say 'I came to my senses'.

> **the senses only work in the present**, and again there is a phrase that captures it – on seeing things for what they are, we say **'I came to my senses'**

One illustration of really waking up is the fight-or-flight response (for example, driving 'asleep' until there is an emergency). There is a surge in adrenaline and cortisol from the activation of the pituitary-adrenal axis, the mind clears and we are ready for action. This is not stress, and adrenaline and cortisol are not stress hormones – they are simply hormones doing their job. However, when their elevation is prolonged there is the potential for damage to the cardiovascular and immune systems, and they can be sustained by merely ruminating about the emotional upset – hence the definition of stress as being preoccupied with emotional upset. This is why pressure is not stress. Pressure is an increase in demand, and body and mind are aroused to deal with it. This only becomes a problem if that arousal is maintained, instead of letting go of the emotional upset that feeds rumination.

This is why the analogy of catching monkeys is so apt for the training. Just like the inconsequential idea that we latch onto and ruminate about, at great cost to mind and body, the monkey gives up his life by gripping the peanut instead of letting go. Another analogy used in the programme is the house with two doors as a model for the mind. The diagrams describe three ways of dealing with upset. The first two, denial and becoming lost in rumination, are maladaptive. In both cases, the outcome is the same. The third way is to use detachment, which in this context means being able to see things for what they are – molehills remain molehills. The house analogy was used to encapsulate the four steps to freedom from stress: waking up, controlling attention, becoming detached, and letting go.

The stress management techniques described here can also be applied to communication skills. Session 7 described a conventional approach to learning how to communicate more effectively, based on a 'tool kit' of communicative behaviours with rules for using them. The flaw in this model is that strategies such as eye contact are impossible to prescribe in simple percentages. Skilled communicators will vary eye contact, depending on who they're talking to and what they're talking about. A different approach is to assume that everyone can communicate effectively, but only when they are awake and controlling attention.

A final step was then added which modified the detached coping of stress management to detaching

the consequence is that anything said about work is taken to be aimed at me personally, and both myself and the work have become the target. Instead, the person needs to be detached from the work

people from their roles. This is particularly important of our work role, with which we easily become identified. The consequence is that anything said about work is taken to be aimed at me personally, and both myself and the work have become the target. Instead, the person needs to be detached from the work, so that evaluations of the work can be made without them being taken as personal criticisms.

The final part of the book was devoted to relaxation. At the outset, it was acknowledged that learning physical relaxation will offer only short-term benefits, and although useful, it needs to be coupled with relaxing the mind.

It should also be acknowledged that no single training programme will answer all needs. It is important for employees to be equipped to deal personally with stress in a proactive and preventative way, but there might be simple practical problems with the management structure that should be addressed in tandem. The Challenge of Change programme has the advantage of being compatible with most of these systems, and the two approaches – personal and structural – should be seen as complementary rather than comprehensive in their own right.

Part of the wider context into which this book fits includes lifestyle issues as well as organisational structure. For example, diet and exercise should form part of a comprehensive effort to manage stress, though always within a view to achieving a balance. Where diet is concerned, it is easy to fall victim to every new piece of evidence that emerges, some of which is contradictory! In principle, moderation is the best strategy, and this applies to alcohol consumption as well – there is growing evidence to suggest that a moderate amount of alcohol can actually be quite healthy. In the same way, there are undoubted benefits from exercise, but it is easy to overstretch yourself and lose sight of the aim, particularly if it becomes an incessant competition to beat everyone (including your own last performance) rather than being a pleasure. Other social factors include the use of social supports – the network of people on whom you can rely, and most importantly, to whom you can express emotion. If the network of family and friends is not avail-

> if the network of family and friends is not available, there should be **no stigma attached to seeking formal social support**, in the form of **counselling or support groups**

able, there should be no stigma attached to seeking formal social support, in the form of counselling or support groups.

Apart from the habitual ways we have learned to behave, and which may make us more or less vulnerable to stress, we are also born with genetic susceptibilities. Indeed, these may have an overriding influence on our health that no amount of stress management can offset. However, these are largely unknown future possibilities – the most important place to be is here in the present. It is here that we seek and maintain the balance in the loft of the mind depicted in our house diagram, and the steps that the diagram illustrates are essentially simple. There is no doubt that it easier to describe than to do – it takes sustained practice to break habits. However, the evidence is clear that with practice it does work, and the benefit of a happier life provides all the incentive we need.

the challenge of change profile

instructions

The Profile offers the opportunity to assess your own strengths and weaknesses in relation to stress. For each of the questions below, please circle either TRUE or FALSE. You should not spend too long on each question – try to respond as quickly as you can, answering in the direction that you would typically tend to behave. If you feel that an item is neither entirely true nor false, please choose the alternative that is most like you. If you haven't been in the situation described, please say how you feel you would behave in that situation.

The scoring will provide scores based on the three scales, labelled R, E-I and DET. What these codes stand for, and the interpretation of the scores, is provided on the final page.

Provided you answer honestly, without trying to cast yourself in the most favourable light, the Profile will provide an assessment of your behaviour that has been extensively validated by the ongoing research programme being carried out by the author. There are three separate scales in the questionnaire. The scoring instructions are provided at the end, and each scale ranges from a minimum of zero to a maximum of 10. However, it is important to remember:

● It is impossible to assess anyone's personality with 100% accuracy. For example, something particular may have happened to you just prior to answering the questions, and this experience may well bias your reply to one or more specific questions. For this reason, where a high score is preferable, it does not mean the maximum of 10 – a high score is interpreted here as ranging from 8 to 10. In the same way, a low score means not just zero, but a range from zero to 2.

● It is also important to remember that these are habitual behaviours, and can therefore be changed – they are not fixed, other than by force of habit. While there will undoubtedly be some genetic or biological contribution to the behaviour, the genetic influence is likely to be small.

- The aim of the profile is provide a concise summary of the way you typically behave, and where the score is in the less preferred direction, that will indicate to you an area of your behaviour in response to stress that needs to be changed. These habits are not easily modified, but with practice you can make a great deal of difference.
- Once you have read the above instructions, please complete the questions, using the scoring instructions at the end to arrive at your score. A brief summary of what the scales mean is on the final page.

the profile

1. When things are not going right, I tend to criticise or blame myself.	TRUE FALSE
2. I often find myself thinking over and over about things that make me angry.	TRUE FALSE
3. Some people need somebody to confide in but I prefer to solve my own problems.	TRUE FALSE
4. When I'm under stress, I tend to feel lonely or isolated.	TRUE FALSE
5. I don't bear a grudge - when something is over, it's over, and I don't think about it again.	TRUE FALSE
6. When I feel upset about something I usually feel the need to talk to someone about it.	TRUE FALSE
7. Sometimes I get so involved thinking about upsetting things I am unable to feel positive about the future.	TRUE FALSE
8. I think you have to keep things in proportion – nothing is really that important.	TRUE FALSE
9. I get worked up just thinking about things that upset me in the past.	TRUE FALSE
10. When something upsets me I prefer to talk to someone about it than to bottle it up.	TRUE FALSE
11. When things are bad, I usually decide it's useless to get upset and just get on with it.	TRUE FALSE

12.	Sometimes I am unable to confide even in someone who is close to me.	TRUE FALSE
13.	Any reminder about upsetting things brings all the emotion flooding back.	TRUE FALSE
14.	Under stress, I become irritable or angry.	TRUE FALSE
15.	I don't let a lot of unimportant things irritate me.	TRUE FALSE
16.	I seldom show how I feel about things.	TRUE FALSE
17.	I often feel overpowered and at the mercy of difficult situations.	TRUE FALSE
18.	When things get tough I try to keep a sense of humour, and laugh at myself or the situation.	TRUE FALSE
19.	I seldom get preoccupied with worries about my future.	TRUE FALSE
20.	I have friends who I know would help me with problems but I would find it difficult to ask.	TRUE FALSE
21.	I can usually see situations for what they actually are and nothing more.	TRUE FALSE
22.	It doesn't make me feel vulnerable if I have to ask other people for help.	TRUE FALSE
23.	I worry less about what might happen than most people I know.	TRUE FALSE
24.	I don't feel embarrassed or anxious about expressing my feelings.	TRUE FALSE
25.	I usually resolve issues by not becoming identified with them.	TRUE FALSE
26.	I am afraid that if I confide in someone they will tell my problems to others.	TRUE FALSE

27. I often feel as if I'm just waiting for something bad to happen.	TRUE	FALSE
28. If I receive bad news in front of others I usually try to hide how I feel.	TRUE	FALSE
29. When I'm under pressure, I tend to see problems or situations as threats.	TRUE	FALSE
30. Intrusive thoughts about problems I'm going to have to deal with make it difficult for me to keep my mind on a task.	TRUE	FALSE

scoring the profile

your scores

R: 1 point for TRUE for 2, 7, 9, 13, 27, 30
and 1 point for FALSE for 5, 15, 19, 23.

R:

E-I: 1 point for TRUE for 3, 12, 16, 20, 26, 28
and 1 point for FALSE for 6, 10, 22, 24.

E-I:

DET: 1 point for TRUE for 8, 11, 18, 21, 25
and 1 point for FALSE for 1, 4, 14, 17, 29.

DET:

interpreting the scores

In the scoring above:

R stands for **rumination**. This measures the tendency to ruminate about emotion-ally upsetting events that have occurred in the past or might occur in the future. While this preoccupation continues attention cannot be given to anything else, and work must inevitably suffer. Furthermore, ruminating has the effect of main-taining physiological arousal, so that levels of hormones such as cortisol and adrenaline remain high; hence the lower the score the better.

E-I stands for **emotional inhibition**. This scale measures the tendency to inhibit the expression of emotional experiences. Expressing emotion can have the effect of reducing the personal burden of emotional upset by sharing it with others. Low scores are consequently preferable, although the expression of emotion must always take account of time and place. This scale is independent of the first one,

ℹ︎

but the combined effects of inhibiting emotion and persistently ruminating over emotional upset may be particularly strongly associated with stress.

DET stands for **detached coping**. High scores here indicate the ability to keep things in perspective: molehills remain molehills and don't become mountains. It is not, however, a measure of emotional coldness. Rather, it describes a strategy of being able to see things in perspective. Low scores may indicate a tendency to become overwhelmed by negative emotion, and high scores are therefore preferable.

references

Asterita, M.F. (1985) *The Physiology of Stress.* N.Y.: Human Sciences Press.

Cameron, R. and Meichenbaum, D. (1982) The nature of effective coping and the treatment of stress related problems: A cognitive-behavioral perspective. In *Handbook of Stress* (Eds. L. Goldberger and S. Bernitz), New York: Free Press.

Monat, A. and Lazarus, R.S. (1991) *Stress & Coping (3rd Edition).* New York: Columbia University Press.

Roger, D. and Hudson, C. (1995) The role of emotion control and emotional rumination in stress management training. *International Journal of Stress Management* 2, 119–132.

Roger, D., Jarvis, G. and Najarian, B. (1993) Detachment and coping: The construction and validation of a new scale for measuring coping strategies. *Personality and Individual Differences* 15, 619–626.

Roger, D. and Jamieson, J. (1988) Individual differences in delayed heart-rate recovery following stress: The role of extraversion, neuroticism and emotional control. *Personality and Individual Differences* 9, 721–726.

Roger, D. and Najarian, B. (1989) The construction and validation of a new scale for measuring emotional control. *Personality and Individual Differences* 10, 845–853.

Roger, D. & Najarian, B. (1998) The relationship between emotional rumination and cortisol secretion under stress. *Personality & Individual Differences* 24, 531–538.

Roger, D. and Schapals, T. Repression-sensitization and emotion control. *Current Psychology* (in press).

Schroeder, D.H. and Costa, P.T. (1984) Influence of life event stress on physical illness. *Journal of Personality & Social Behaviour* 46, 853–863.

index